To Save This
State From Ruin

ERRATUM

p. 18, line 15: £5 should be £50.

To Save This State From Ruin

New Jersey and the Creation of the United States Constitution, 1776–1789

Mary R. Murrin

Trenton
New Jersey Historical Commission, Department of State

Copyright © 1987 by the New Jersey Historical Commission,
Department of State
All rights reserved
Printed in the United States of America

New Jersey Historical Commission, Department of State
113 West State Street, CN 305
Trenton, NJ 08625

Thomas H. Kean, Governor
Jane Burgio, Secretary of State

Library of Congress Cataloging in Publication Data

Murrin, Mary R.
 To save this state from ruin.

 Bibliography: p.
 1. New Jersey—History—Revolution, 1775–1783.
 2. New Jersey—history—1775–1865. 3. United States—Constitutional history. I. Title.
 F137.M88 1987   974.9'03   86-33327
 ISBN 0-89743-103-0

For Mother and Jenny

Contents

Acknowledgments	ix
To Save This State From Ruin	3
1 A Common and Mutual Interest	4
2 People, Politics and the Economy	13
3 Postwar Dilemmas and Controversies	27
4 New Jersey in the New Nation	51
5 Toward A New Nation	64
Chronology	86
Notes	93
Bibliographical Essay	95

Acknowledgments

I am grateful to a number of people for their assistance with this project.

Many Commission staff members made useful contributions. Howard L. Green, Richard Waldron, Lee R. Parks, and Bernard Bush all read the manuscript. David S. Cohen provided information about material culture for the illustration captions. Nancy H. Dallaire handled design and production.

Most of all I want to thank John Murrin, who read the manuscript at every stage of its development and was generous with encouragement and important suggestions.

To Save This
State From Ruin

To Save This State From Ruin

At the close of the revolutionary war, New Jersey faced most of the same difficulties besetting other states. However, internal differences complicated the state's response to problems of debtor-creditor relations, currency, and the Continental debt. Distinctive patterns of ethnicity, trade, land use and religion first established during the proprietary period when New Jersey was two colonies were still evident. The two regions, East and West Jersey, were at loggerheads on possible solutions to these postwar problems. But a decade of experience trying to resolve them made the state as a whole receptive to the Constitution. New Jerseyans believed the Articles of Confederation to be seriously flawed and were united on two major issues troubling the new nation—the disposition of western lands and Congress's need for a secure income. The Constitution answered the state's several objections to the Articles, but the period of unanimity was brief. New Jerseyans were wrangling again by the first federal election as sectional antagonisms resumed their place in New Jersey politics.

1

A Common and Mutual Interest

The Articles of Confederation, placed before the states for ratification in late 1777, for the most part continued the constitutional relationships established under the Continental Congress. However, the text was far more explicit in giving ultimate sovereignty to the states. The central government had narrow, specific powers, and the states retained authority over all those powers not enumerated. The Confederation Congress had no power to tax, impose import duties or, except by treaty, regulate trade. Under the Articles, and indeed after 1779, Congress no longer met its expenses simply by printing paper money. All governmental expenses, such as those required by the prosecution of a bitter war and later the servicing of the Continental debt, depended upon a system of requisition. Congress met its expenses by assessing each state a quota of the total amount required. Managing the war, coining and borrowing money, and making treaties and alliances required the assent of nine of the thirteen states. Any amendment to the Articles required the assent of all thirteen states.

The New Jersey legislature made its position on the Confederation quite clear in 1778. On June 16 the legislature sent a "Representation" to the Continental Congress listing a number of objections to the proposed Articles of Confederation and urging their revision. The memorial New Jersey submitted emphasized issues of revenue, trade regulation, and western lands—topics of great importance during the next decade.

The legislature's memorial called for fixed state boundaries within five years, argued that Congress should have sole authority to regulate trade and impose customs duties, and observed that Congress should have authority over western lands so that all states might benefit rather than a few. On this last point the legislature observed plaintively,

> the present War ... was undertaken for the general Defence and Interest of the confederating Colonies.... It was ever the confident Expectation of this State, that the Benefits derived from a successful Contest were to be general and proportionate.... [The states] have fought and bled for it [Crown land] in Proportion to their respective Abilities, and therefore the Reward ought not to be predilectionally distributed. Shall such States as are shut out by Situation from availing themselves of the least Advantage from this Quarter, be left to sink under an enormous Debt, whilst others are enabled in a short Period to replace all their Expenditures from the hard Earnings of the whole Confederacy?[1]

Congress listened, but it rejected the proposed revisions. In July, New Jersey delegate Nathaniel Scudder wrote to John Hart, the speaker of the New Jersey assembly, urging the legislature to direct its delegates to ratify the Articles, despite any disadvantage to the state. He pointed out that small states could be at a severe disadvantage if Congress began amending the Articles. Warning of the "fatal Consequences" should the Articles not be ratified and America be revealed as a "Rope of Sand," Scudder asserted that "every State must expect to be subjected to considerable local Disadvantages in a general Confederation."[2] In November, still convinced the Articles needed substantial revision, the New Jersey legislature relented. New Jersey was the eleventh state to ratify, followed in 1779 and 1781 by Delaware and Maryland, two other small states which objected to the absence of any provision for the western lands.

A Common and Mutual Interest

New Jersey's objections were understandable. New Jersey had no means to satisfy Congress's requisitions except by taxing its citizens. A small state with fixed boundaries, it had no western lands, no real port and negligible foreign trade. Its merchants shipped their goods through the ports of Philadelphia and New York City. Both New York and Pennsylvania exacted import duties on goods shipped from or through New Jersey.

An examination of New Jersey's precarious economic situation and tangled politics at the end of the war makes the state's enthusiasm for a more powerful central government comprehensible.

A Troubled and Divided State

The bloodshed, strife and bitterness of the Revolution was both an unfamiliar and unwelcome experience. The state had escaped Indian raids and the clash of armies in the French and Indian War. Except for a number of land riots, New Jerseyans remained relatively peaceful throughout the colonial period. Few were prepared for the agonies of armed conflict. In June 1776 Elias Boudinot, a whig who viewed the conflict with Britain with regret and alarm, had warned

> Soon as We Declare for Independancy, every prospect of Peace must Vanish. Ruthless War, with all it's aggravated horrors, will Ravage our Once happy Land; our Sea Coasts & Ports will be Ruined & our Ships taken as Pyrates; Torrints of Blood be Spilt, & thousands reduc'd to beggery & wretchedness.[3]

Boudinot's words were prophetic. New Jersey was devastated by the war. The British marched back and forth across the state twice, pursuing Americans or being pursued by them. New Jersey was the scene of more military engagements than any other state. Bergen, Essex, Middlesex and Somerset coun-

A Common and Mutual Interest

ties in East Jersey and Burlington County in West Jersey received the most attention from the competing armies; Monmouth County was the scene of vicious patriot-loyalist struggles. In 1782 the New Jersey legislature ordered a survey of the damages inflicted by both armies. The finished work filled six volumes. Five volumes detailed the two thousand incidents of destruction (average loss £100 specie) involving British troops, and a sixth listed the instances credited to American troops. The catalogue of damage was appalling, but the victims received no compensation.

The contending armies brought destruction whether they were camping, marching or fighting. Armies stole, trampled and confiscated. Food and firewood were essential; cold and hungry soldiers cared little about questions of ownership. Wooden fences were raw material for firewood; chickens, geese, pigs and cattle were candidates for the food pot. Destruction of farmers' fences allowed cattle to stray, trampling any crops still standing. In an economy of small family farms, the presence of armies was disastrous.

Farmers received payment for only a portion of their losses—mainly food and material requisitioned by the commissary and quartermaster departments. By 1779–80, when currency problems reached their height, federal officers issued certificates, or promises to pay, instead of money. The burden of this form of finance fell most heavily on the states where the war was fought—for this period New Jersey, Pennsylvania and New York. In 1780 New Jersey and its two neighbors each held about $20 million in certificates. These certificates, together with the other forms of Continental and state paper, represented the Continental and state debt. Establishing an equitable value for the array of financial paper and achieving an orderly system of interest payments remained vexing problems for both the Congress and New Jersey in the 1780s.

Skirmishing between patriot and tory exerted its own toll. New Jersey had a substantial loyalist population, about

51,000 persons or 35 percent of the white population. The conflicts between loyalists and patriots were frequently ugly. Nicholas Collins, a Swedish Lutheran minister, described the "Civil War" raging in Gloucester County.

> Everywhere distrust, fear, hatred and abominable selfishness were met with. Parents and children, brothers and sisters, wife and husband were enemies to one another. The militia and some regular troops on one side and refugees with the Englishmen on the other were constantly roving about in smaller or greater numbers, plundering and destroying everything in a barbarous manner, cattle, furniture, clothing and food; they smashed mirrors, tables and china, etc., and plundered women and children of their most necessary clothing, cut up the bolsters and scattered the feathers to the wind, burned houses, whipped and imprisoned each other, and surprised people when they were deep asleep.[4]

Maintaining a more neutral stance frequently proved impossible. James Moody, a Sussex County farmer who described himself as "no politician," fled to British lines in April 1777 when his efforts to avoid conflict with his neighbors failed. Moody, in a lengthy and bitter third-person narrative, complained that

> The general cry was, *Join or die!* Mr. Moody relished neither of these alternatives, and therefore remained on his farm a silent, but not unconcerned, spectator.... It was in vain that he took every possible precaution, consistent with a good conscience, not to give offence. Some infatuated associations were very near consigning him to the latter of these alternatives, only because neither his judgment, nor his conscience, would suffer him to adopt the former.... Finding it impossible either to convince these associators, or to be convinced by them, any longer stay among them was useless; and an attempt made upon him soon after, rendered it impossible.[5]

On the whole, the northern part of the state endured the heaviest fighting and suffered the most damage. Most of New Jersey's five hundred confiscated loyalist estates were in the north, as were most of those who had supported the war with money and goods and consequently now held most of New Jersey's state and federal debt. The region's social and economic structure was in considerable disarray. Ebenezer Hazard, postmaster of New York, recorded his observations on the destruction in a diary kept during a trek through central New Jersey in 1777.

> Great Devastation was made by the Enemy at Somerset Court House: The Dutch and Presbyterian Churches (framed Buildings) were stripped of their Pulpits & Pews, their Doors & Windows were broken, & the Boards torn off the Outside, so as to leave the Frames bare. Several Dwelling Houses were destroyed;—the Thatch was torn off of Barns & Barracks.[6]

The southern part of the state was plagued by bandits and tory raiding parties, particularly when the British held Philadelphia. However, the region saw little military action and escaped most of the destruction associated with the war as well as its economic consequences. The Quakers who dominated the region were unenthusiastic about armed resistance, refused to pay taxes to support the war and declined to accept the paper money which had been issued during the conflict.

The imbalance reinforced New Jersey's traditional economic and cultural divisions, a legacy of the colonial period.

The Two Jerseys

From 1676 to 1702, most of the proprietary period, New Jersey was actually two colonies. Each had a board of proprietors which retained political authority and title to much of the land. The dividing line between the proprietary colonies of East and West Jersey ran from a point on the upper Delaware in northwest New Jersey down to Little Egg Harbor. Since the exact location of the point on the Delaware was in dispute the precise location of the dividing line re-

mained in contention. In 1702 the two boards of proprietors, unable to govern effectively, surrendered their political power to the Crown, and East and West Jersey became a single royal colony.

In 1780 most of New Jersey's population lived on the fertile lands of the Delaware watershed and along waterways flowing into Newark and Raritan bays. The corridor from Philadelphia to New York was somewhat more densely settled than other areas in the state and contained most of New Jersey's larger towns. No town boasted more than fifteen hundred inhabitants. Despite the state's overall rural character, East and West Jersey exhibited important differences.

Dutch, English, Scots-Irish, Irish and Germans made up the bulk of East Jersey's white population. Most of the state's blacks, the majority of them slaves, lived in the north, especially in Bergen and Somerset counties. Four of the state's six largest towns—Newark, Elizabeth Town, Perth Amboy and New Brunswick—were in East Jersey.

Economically, East Jersey was in New York City's orbit. It was a region of small family farms, averaging about eighty acres, which produced little for sale. The limited acreage

An Original Sketch of New Brunswick, New Jersey, Taken Just After the Revolution, by Archibald Robertson. Emmet Collection, Prints Division, The New York Public Library, Astor, Lenox and Tilden Foundations.

This drawing shows a fairly densely settled town. The Dutch influence is clear. The Dutch architectural style of the church in the foreground contrasts with the English style of the newer Episcopal church in the left background. This type of Dutch architecture has disappeared from the landscape. The rather narrow town houses, the unpaved streets, and the extensive use of wood in many of the buildings and in the post-and-rail and palisade fencing are typical of the period. The ships' masts in the right background indicate New Brunswick's status as a port.

meant that East Jersey did not have many artisans or laborers. Land was reasonably well distributed—10 percent of the population owned one-third of the land, a pattern that is highly egalitarian. Only 1 percent of the population owned over five hundred acres. About 30 percent of the male population was landless, a group which included artisans, farm laborers, some professionals and merchants. A few small manufactories, some iron works in Bergen, Monmouth, Sussex and Hunterdon counties, and tradesmen and shopkeepers in the few urban areas completed the economic picture.

In religion, most of the population was English Calvinist or Dutch Reformed, with lesser numbers of Episcopalians (Anglicans). A disproportionately large number of the revolutionary leaders were Presbyterian. Significant numbers of Anglicans and Dutch Reformed were either neutrals or loyalists.

West Jersey's population was more homogeneous. While there were a few Germans, Finns and Swedes, most of the people were English. The area was dominated by the Quakers, who generally opposed both armed resistance and the taxes which made it possible. West Jersey was more rural, had slightly larger farms, and was somewhat more prosperous. On the whole, southwestern New Jersey had many more five-hundred-acre farms than the counties around New York. Land was not as well distributed in West Jersey as East. For example, 10 percent of the Burlington County taxpayers owned half of the land. Salem and Gloucester counties showed the same pattern. As much as 50 percent of the population was landless. Better land and larger farms made it possible to produce crops for sale. This kind of community generated more artisans, more laborers, more professionals, and a larger commercial sector. Economically, West Jersey looked to Philadelphia. Two of the state's six largest towns, Trenton and Burlington, were in West Jersey.

2

People, Politics and the Economy

The Economy

In the 1780s New Jersey was an agricultural state; between 70 and 80 percent of the state's population of 150,000 owed its living in some way to the land. Roughly half of the state's population were landowners of one sort or another. Another one-third were laborers (including 10 percent indentured servants and 4 percent slaves). Most of these could expect to acquire a farm at some point. Another 10 percent were artisans and another 4–5 percent were either professionals or engaged in commerce. The wealthiest 10 percent owned about 45 percent of the farm property.

Information about the specifics of New Jersey's economy between 1776 and 1789 is scanty, but we do know something about the overall pattern of the middle Atlantic area. There was some manufacturing, generally on the household level. During slack seasons farmers cut lumber and made shingles. Gristmill operators, whose products were tied to the growing season, frequently ran country stores or operated sawmills. Craftsmen also worked at home, and their families often helped in the production of goods. Mills of all kinds (textile, saw, grist), distilleries, and furnace industries were among the list of manufacturers. New Jersey was a leading source of

American iron and also produced glass, sawmill and textile products, flour and other foodstuffs.

The general contraction of the 1780s affected the entire American economy. The West Indies had been a major market for food and timber products and draft animals, but the war severed direct trade links. There had been some compensatory trade during the war with both the French islands and the Spanish colonies, but the Spanish and British governments closed their colonies to American shipping following the war. Efforts to find new outlets were hampered by the difficulty of securing commercial agreements.

Small-scale manufacturers who had prospered during the war adapted poorly to the peace. British goods, once more available, were of higher quality and cheaper besides. American merchants restocked their shelves on credit and then found few customers for their goods. Speculators who had exploited the easy credit of an inflationary wartime economy fell into debt as the economy contracted. Crop failures brought hardship to New Jersey farmers already in difficulty from wartime destruction, debt and high taxes. Many iron forges and furnaces failed. The number of lawsuits for recovery of debt rose rapidly.

View Near Kingston, New Jersey. Pencil drawing from a sketchbook (1792–1802) by Thomas Russell. Historical Society of Pennsylvania.

The kind of mixed agricultural enterprise common in late eighteenth-century New Jersey is well represented in this sketch. The view is of Kingston looking toward Princeton. Note the mill, the farm animals (cattle on the left of the road, sheep on the right), and the regular arrangement of trees indicating orchards. The road by the mill is probably present-day Route 27; it was the major transportation route between Perth Amboy and Trenton.

Government and Politics

In most ways the state constitution of 1776 was a response to New Jersey's experience as a royal colony. Annual elections, the right to set its own adjournment, the regulation of fees, and the control of money bills had been on the assembly's agenda during much of the colonial period. The document clearly portrays the distrust of executive authority.

In a structure that included a governor, legislative council and general assembly, the assembly was predominant. Assembly and council in joint session selected the man who would serve as both governor and president of the council; they also chose all the judges of the supreme and inferior courts, the justices of the peace, the attorney-general, the secretary of state, and the state treasurer. Since the assembly had three times the membership of the council, it had the

Pryor's Mill, Near Point of Rocks. From Charles H. Winfield, History of the County of Hudson *(1874).*

This drawing (probably from the nineteenth century) shows a late eighteenth-century grain mill near Paulus Hook (now Jersey City). The difference between the water levels on the right and left of the picture indicates a dam. This mill is apparently of the undershot type, in which water flows under the wheel rather than over it. The vehicle that has just delivered grain to the mill is a "Jersey farm wagon," commonly used for light hauling. Note the two millstones leaning against the building and the man carrying the grain sack. Schooners like the one shown here were typically used for shipping grain and other commodities along the coast and up the rivers to their natural or manmade fall lines. The church steeple in the background is the only evidence of the settlement of Paulus Hook; steeples, the tallest structures in most towns, were major landmarks.

more powerful voice in the selection of state officials. The assembly chose its own officers, determined its members' qualifications, had the power to authorize its speaker to call a special session, and decided on its own adjournment. Assembly and council passed all laws, but the assembly alone initiated all money bills. Three restrictions were placed on the assembly: it could not abolish annual elections or trial by jury, and it could not infringe the free exercise of religion.

There was a property requirement for election to the legislative council and assembly, but rampant inflation made the requirement less onerous than it had been under royal government. Men of moderate means served in New Jersey's legislature. While there was a property requirement for the franchise, it was not particularly stringent. Extending the vote to citizens with £5 worth of property broadened the electorate to include many voters of modest means.

Some scholars have argued that the constitution's provision permitting women and free blacks to vote was simply an oversight. However, in 1790 New Jersey adopted an election law explicitly referring to voters as he or she, and in 1800 it rejected a law extending female suffrage to congressional elections on the grounds of redundancy. Alas, this democratic experiment was short-lived. In 1807, blaming a fraud-ridden election on the nearest scapegoats, women and free blacks, the legislature disfranchised both.

The council acted as an advisory body to the governor as well as the upper house of the legislature. Governor and council together constituted the court of errors and appeals. The governor's power was sharply reduced from what his royal predecessors had enjoyed. The governor had no appointive power or veto and he was dependent upon the assembly for his salary. Though he was the commander-in-chief of the state militia, his most significant function was judicial, since he presided over the state's highest court, the court of errors and appeals. Constitutionally, he was little more than a figure-

People, Politics and the Economy

head, though William Livingston, the first to hold the office, demonstrated how much power a clever and strong-willed governor might exert.

The civil disruption accompanying the invasion of the state in 1776 placed an enormous strain on the new state government. William Livingston's efforts to galvanize the state in support of the war effort persuaded the legislature to pass an act in March 1777 delegating some of its powers to the executive. On March 15, 1777, the legislature established the New Jersey Council of Safety, which Livingston headed, to deal with military and civil emergencies, the breakdown of local justice, and the loyalist problem. The council of safety lasted throughout the war.

Politically, New Jersey presented a rich and interesting tapestry. Before the Revolution, 44 percent of those elected to the assembly were large landowners, 18–26 percent were farmers (large and small), 15 percent were professionals (mostly lawyers), and 12 percent were merchants. Postwar New Jersey elected fewer large landowners and doubled the number of farmers. Between 1779 and 1788 New Jersey elected 150 representatives. Property qualifications to hold office were moderate; one-third of the representatives had small estates. An equal percentage could be classed as well-off. Overall, about 46 percent were farmers and another 6 percent were large landowners. Professionals and merchants made up 15 percent and 14 percent respectively of the legislature. About 14 percent of the group could be classed as miscellaneous nonfarmers (small manufacturers, artisans), and the rest could not be identified by occupation.

The different wartime experience and economic situation of the two regions influenced voting patterns on some issues. Representatives of the East Jersey counties of Monmouth, Middlesex, Somerset, Bergen, Essex and Morris often voted as a block during the 1770s and 1780s. Hunterdon County's legislators tended to vote with this group. On the whole, East

Jersey representatives supported any measure favoring debtors and opposed measures requiring the expenditure of funds. The West Jersey group included representatives from Burlington, Gloucester, Salem, Cumberland and Cape May. West Jersey legislators, often wealthier than their East Jersey counterparts and with fewer debtors among their constituents, opposed measures favoring debtors. During the war, Sussex County's legislators, because of the county's loyalist population, voted with West Jersey. After the war, when economic issues predominated, its legislators switched to the East Jersey side.

Social and Cultural Context

All citizens did not share equally in the new society proclaimed by the Declaration of Independence. Most blacks remained enslaved, and women had few legal rights.

New Jersey had a large Afro-American population, which contributed significantly to the state's economy. Most black men did some kind of agricultural work, but in slack times their white masters frequently assigned them other tasks or sold their labor to other masters. New Jersey's economy, though primarily agricultural, was more diversified than the plantation economy of the South. Afro-Americans worked as hunters, farmers, blacksmiths and carpenters. They tended livestock, labored in forges and in mines, cut timber and worked wood. Blacks served on both sides of the revolutionary war, but independence brought those who served the patriot cause little benefit. Very few gained freedom as recompense for their service in the cause of American liberty. For many the war's aftermath brought ill fortune. White slaveowners, in debt and squeezed by the postwar depression, sold their slaves to new masters.

New Jersey Quakers directed several petitions on slaveholding to the legislature in the 1780s. Despite influential support from Livingston, congressional delegate William Churchill Houston, and newspapermen Isaac Collins and Shepard Kollock, the legislature took no action until 1786, when it authorized the manumission of slaves and forbade their importation or abuse. Not satisfied, the Quakers renewed their efforts, and the legislature responded with a stronger law in 1788. The new act provided for the forfeiture of any ship involved in the slave trade, forbade a slave's forcible removal from the state unless accompanied by his master, required the same court proceedings and criminal penalties for blacks and whites, and required masters to teach their slaves to read. Quaker efforts succeeded in ameliorating the condition of enslaved blacks, but abolition was still a generation away.

New York and Rhode Island, two other northern states with significant black populations, abolished slavery earlier than New Jersey. The real or imagined threat from free blacks or slaves flocking to the British cause during the Revolution undoubtedly contributed to white New Jerseyans' fear and distrust of blacks. This fear was especially prevalent in northern New Jersey, which harbored a significant population of both blacks and loyalists. The climate of distrust, slaveholders' economic investment in slaves, and the widespread belief that blacks were inferior beings not entitled to the basic rights trumpeted by the Declaration of Independence put abolition far into the future. In 1810 New Jersey was the only northern state with more slaves than free blacks.

A woman's experience during the war was largely determined by the activities or political stance of her husband or father. In her husband's absence, a woman tended the farm or shop alone. In the eighteenth century a married woman was legally and actually dependent on her husband. She might express her opinions on politics, the war, and other subjects privately. She had no public voice and little freedom of action. A woman married to a loyalist, whether she shared her husband's political opinions or not, followed her husband and lost her friends, her home and her place in society.

The Revolution changed the woman's role in subtle ways. Legally, her position did not change. Few women owned property. Married women could not control money. Women exercised little political influence. New Jersey did permit women and free blacks to vote for a brief period, but it is difficult to tell how many exercised the privilege.

Independence brought women a variety of social benefits but little political power. Theirs was not the public stage of politics or the professions, but the private arena of the home. As the economy changed and men began to work away from the home, domestic concerns, including the nurturing and education of republican sons for a republican society, became the exclusive responsibility of women. Educational opportunities for women broadened in the late eighteenth and early nineteenth century, and this period is associated with a dramatic increase in female literacy. Activities outside the home which drew women were in "feminine" areas. In increasing numbers, women became schoolmistresses and formed female benevolent societies. Later they played important roles in evangelical religious and antislavery societies.

Organized religion and educational institutions fared poorly during the war. All religious denominations paid a heavy price for the war, but Presbyterians, Quakers and Anglicans may have suffered more than most. All three experienced a decrease in the number of churches or meetings in the postrevolutionary war era. Presbyterians made significant contributions to the revolutionary cause in New Jersey, supplying both civil and military leaders. Energies directed to politics and war left little opportunity for attention to church affairs. Quakers, because of their pacifism, were frequently suspected of toryism. Anglicans fared very poorly. The number of Anglican churches and priests dropped dramatically after the war. Many Anglicans were tories; both laity and ministers left the state in great numbers. Independence severed the organizational ties with England, and the process of reestablishing the church as Episcopal produced much strife.

Both the College of New Jersey and Queen's College, the two institutions of higher learning in New Jersey, were decimated by the events of the 1770s and 1780s. Both institutions (and the towns of Princeton and New Brunswick) were ill-used by Continental and British troops. Studies were interrupted and the numbers of graduates fell. Both revived slowly after the war. Ebenezer Hazard's description of Princeton's plight was vivid.

> Princeton looks like the Picture of Desolation. Several Houses have been burned there: Not a Pew is left in the Meeting House, & a large Brick Chimney has been built where the Pulpit stood; the Windows of this House have all been broken. The College is in a very ruinous Situation, but this suffered more from the Licentiousness of our own Troops than from the ravages of the Enemy; The latter knocked down a Study in each Room, but the former destroyed the Library, damaged the Orrery, broke down the Pews and Rostrum in the Hall, [and] cut the Pillars which supported the Gallery.... All the Windows of the College are broken, & every room in it looks like a Stable.... There are no fences left in Princeton.[7]

For the College of New Jersey, currency depreciation increased the hardship. President John Witherspoon and the college trustees had invested heavily in loan office certificates. The currency depreciation of the early 1780s left college finances in chaos. Perhaps because of the college's experience, Witherspoon became a prominent opponent of paper money measures.

Educational opportunities increased somewhat following the war. The classical curriculum of Latin, Greek, mathematics, and natural and moral philosophy offered at the College of New Jersey and Queen's College did not change for several decades. Both institutions considered this regimen equally appropriate for the gentleman's son and the young man contemplating a future as a minister, physician, lawyer, public servant or merchant. However, the kind of education available for younger students expanded in the postwar period. The "English" or "common" schools taught reading, writing, spelling and arithmetic to girls and boys of two to fourteen years. The "Latin grammar" schools, restricted to boys, taught a classical curriculum plus mathematics, geography and history. Their students began at nine or ten years. Versions of both types of school had existed in the colonial period. Practices varied according to locality, but the kind of elementary education provided in the common school was available to some girls in the dame schools of the colonial period.

The "academies" could be either day or boarding schools and taught either Latin grammar curricula or English school curricula. Some admitted girls as well as boys; occasionally girls used the same facilities at different hours. The number of female academies grew impressively in the first years of the new republic. For the most part these schools either

Bridge At Paterson, by Alexander Robertson (1795). Historical Society of Pennsylvania.

This romantic scene against the background of the Watchung Mountains pictures a still-pastoral New Jersey in the late eighteenth century. Nature is benign and ordered. Paterson, which began industrializing in the 1790s, is upstream and out of sight. The clothing of the two fishermen reflects the transition from the colonial period to the early national period; knee breeches have been replaced by long pants. In this period people still relied heavily on ferries or fords to cross bodies of water. Bridges like the relatively simple one shown required substantial labor and expertise. Extensive and sophisticated bridge building in America is associated with the construction of canals and railroads in the nineteenth century.

depended on some sort of private support or the students paid tuition.

New Jersey had no continuously published newspaper before the Revolution. Its citizens depended on New York or Philadelphia papers for news. In 1777 Isaac Collins founded the state's first newspaper, the *New-Jersey Gazette,* in Burlington. The same year Shepard Kollock began the *New-Jersey Journal* in Chatham. By 1787 there were four weekly papers, all in East Jersey—the *New-Jersey Journal, and Political Intelligencer* at Elizabeth, the *New Brunswick Gazette, and Weekly Monitor,* the *Princeton Packet,* and the *Trenton Mercury.* The 1780s also saw the launching of such periodicals as the *Christian's Scholar's and Farmer's Magazine.*

A few voluntary associations were established in the 1780s. The Trenton Society for Improvement in Useful Knowledge and the New Jersey Society for Promoting Agriculture, Commerce and the Arts were established in the 1780s. The New Jersey Medical Society revived after a period of inactivity during the war. Interest in the improvement of knowledge spawned circulating libraries as well as associations. Burlington, Trenton and Elizabeth Town all had libraries of one sort or another.

3

Postwar Dilemmas and Controversies

Congress issued its peace terms in August 1779. These included the recognition of independence, British evacuation of all American territories, the maintenance of American rights in northern fisheries and the free navigation of the Mississippi River. The preliminary peace treaty, signed in November 1782, agreed to these terms, including very generous boundaries (basically the present-day United States east of the Mississippi, excepting New Orleans and Florida [see figure 1]). The treaty also required the validation of all debts due creditors of either country and called for Congress to recommend the restoration of the rights and property of the loyalists. Some of these provisions greatly complicated the first years of the new nation. In New Jersey and other states, the clauses dealing with the payment of debts and the treatment of loyalists met with considerable resistance.

While New Jerseyans rebuilt houses, schools and churches and reestablished farms and businesses, the state sought solutions for a number of its special problems. New Jersey's internal difficulties and what it saw as the deficiencies of the Confederation were inextricably bound together. On most of these issues New Jerseyans split on geographical lines, but they shared a common frustration with the weakness of the Confederation.

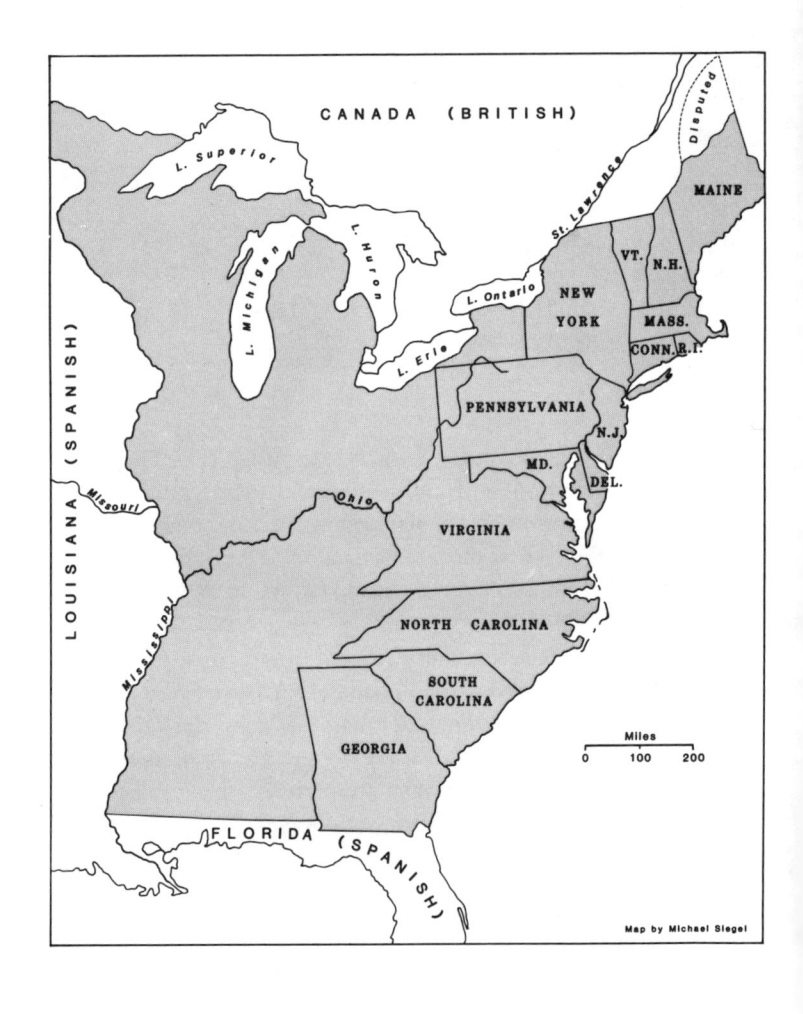

Figure 1. *United States Territory After the Treaty of Paris. Map by Michael Siegel, Center for Coastal and Environmental Studies, Rutgers University.*

The state was beset by six interrelated problems: What should be done about the loyalists? Who had title to several hundred thousand acres of disputed land in northern New Jersey? How should the interests of creditors and debtors be balanced? What should be done about the nagging problem of currency? How were the states and the Congress to pay the vast debt, foreign and domestic, and also meet current expenses? What should the state's attitude be towards the Confederation?

Dominant Political Figures

Three men dominated New Jersey politics in the 1780s—William Livingston, Abraham Clark and William Paterson. Many of the loyalists who fled during the war had been important figures in New Jersey before the war. Their departure both increased Livingston's dominance and opened the door for new figures like Clark and Paterson. Livingston, Clark and Paterson figured prominently in the conflicts surrounding New Jersey's difficulties.

William Livingston

William Livingston (1723-1790) was a member of a prominent New York family. A Yale graduate and lawyer, he achieved eminence in New York public life by wielding an extremely sharp pen. Livingston, a Presbyterian, was a major literary contributor to the controversy surrounding the political and economic role of the Anglican church. In 1772 he abruptly retired to the relative peace of Elizabeth Town, New Jersey.

The retirement was temporary. Livingston became one of New Jersey's delegates to the First and Second Continental congresses and he also served as a general in the New Jersey militia before his selection as the state's first governor in August 1776. He was an ardent patriot and throughout the war he was a scourge to New Jersey's loyalists. Livingston used his position as commander-in-chief of the state militia to wield considerable power and organize New Jersey's defenses, despite the figurehead status prescribed for the governor in the state constitution. In March 1776 the legislature created the New Jersey Council of Safety in an attempt to deal with the breakdown of civil order. Livingston quickly took advantage of his position as head of the council. Most of his efforts were devoted to dealing with the state's serious loyalist problems. In the wartime emergency Livingston's forceful personality and sharp political instincts enabled him to exercise the kind of executive power not envisioned by the men who drafted the state constitution.

Throughout the war and during the Confederation period Livingston made extensive use of his abilities as a polemicist. His "Primitive Whig" essays in 1786 made a forceful case for hard money, labeling debtors as idle spendthrifts and knavish. Livingston's own fortune had been much reduced by the rampant inflation of the 1770s and 1780s, a circumstance which probably reinforced his conservative bent.

In 1787 Livingston served as one of New Jersey's delegates to the Constitutional Convention, but age and ill health limited his contribution. As governor, he supervised the state's first federal election in 1789. The election was marred by considerable fraud, though there is no evidence Livingston was responsible. After the election the composition of New Jersey's congressional delegation remained a subject of dispute for some months. First Livingston and the legislative council considered the election results, and then the matter went to the House of Representatives. It was a somewhat ignominious final act in an illustrious career. Livingston died in July 1790, during his fourteenth term as governor.

Abraham Clark

Abraham Clark (1726–1794) was a figure of signal importance in New Jersey during the 1770s and 1780s. He was one of the signers of the Declaration of Independence and either sat in the New Jersey Assembly or represented New Jersey in Congress for most of the period from 1776 to 1794. Like Livingston, Paterson, and most of the other prominent New Jersey men of the period, Clark lived in the northern part of the state.

There is very little information on Clark's education. His father was a farmer and magistrate, and the family was important in Presbyterian circles. Clark's literary eloquence points to some degree of education, probably home instruction. Though too frail to work in the fields, he always considered himself a farmer. Surveying and transferring land titles were his main occupations, though he also bought and sold land on a small scale.

Clark was a man of fervent republican sympathies and the acknowledged champion of New Jersey's large debtor class. He loathed privilege, distrusted lawyers and had few kind words for merchants. In Clark's eyes, farmers were the true basis of the free and independent society; government's task was to protect its helpless citizens. Clark was the major advocate for paper-money and debtor-relief measures throughout the long years of economic depression. He believed that creditors were economic parasites and speculators were worse. In the larger arena, he feared the economic power of New York and Pennsylvania over New Jersey and favored some expansion of Congress's power.

Clark was selected as one of New Jersey's delegates to the Constitutional Convention but declined to serve, citing his position as congressman. When the Constitution was placed

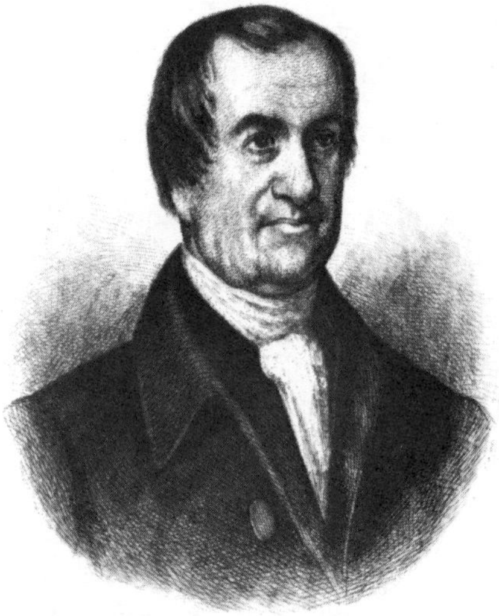

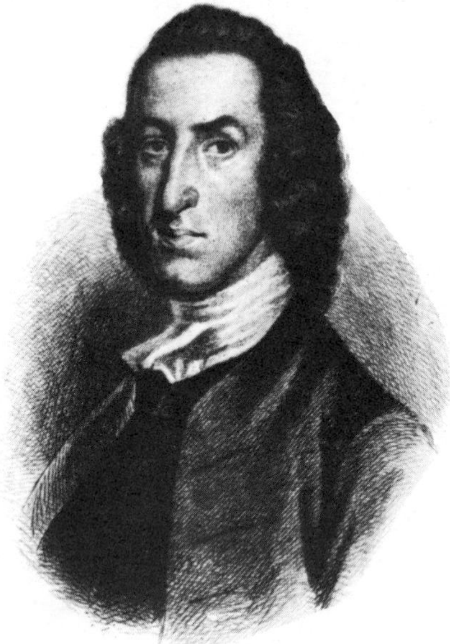

Above, left. *Abraham Clark, by Albert Rosenthal. Emmet Collection, The New York Public Library, Astor, Lenox and Tilden Foundations.*

Left. *William Livingston. Princeton University Archives.*

Above. *William Paterson, by Edward Ludlow Mooney. Special Collections and Archives, Alexander Library, Rutgers University.*

before the Congress, Clark declined to oppose it and voted to forward it to the states without amendment or congressional comment. In other circumstances—perhaps residence in a state without New Jersey's economic problems—Clark might have joined the antifederalist opposition. As it was, he declined to oppose the Constitution.

The hard-money, procreditor forces in New Jersey, which Clark had so antagonized during the 1780s, had their revenge during New Jersey's first federal election in 1789. Most of the shenanigans during this extraordinary election were devoted to denying Clark a congressional seat. The maneuvers were successful, and four opponents of paper money, all staunch Federalists, constituted the state's first congressional delegation. Clark's congressional career was only briefly thwarted. He was elected to Congress in 1791 and served until his death in 1794.

William Paterson

William Paterson (1745–1806) is the third of our prominent New Jersey men of the 1780s. He was a strong nationalist and, like Livingston, a vigorous whig and staunch defender of property. Paterson was born in Ireland and came to America with the rest of his family when he was two. He graduated from the College of New Jersey in 1763 and began a five-year legal apprenticeship with Richard Stockton. Upon completion of his legal training he settled in Raritan, Somerset County. Initial efforts to establish a lucrative legal practice went unrewarded.

In 1775 and 1776 he served as a Somerset County delegate to the New Jersey Provincial Congress, where his capacity for diligence won him recognition. He was reelected to the second Provincial Congress. In 1776 he was chosen attorney-general of the new state, embarked on a vigorous prosecution of loyalists, and established a thriving legal practice. He also served on the legislative council and the council of safety. At war's end he retired from office, turning his attention to his legal practice.

During the 1780s Paterson was heavily involved in two of the hottest and most lucrative issues in New Jersey politics: the dividing-line controversy and the debtor-creditor disputes. Paterson was one of a team of lawyers enlisted by the East Jersey proprietors in their attempt to retain title to a large area of northern New Jersey land. In 1784 Paterson, William Churchill Houston, Robert Morris and John Rutherfurd achieved a victory for the East Jersey side. In this period Paterson was best known as a vigorous defender of creditor interests. A castigator of debtors and a sharp opponent of loan offices, Paterson grew rich through a careful attention to the interests of his creditor clients.

In 1787 he served as one of New Jersey's delegates to the Constitutional Convention. Paterson was a vigorous exponent of the small-state position and a major figure behind the New Jersey plan. Understandably alarmed at the power given large states by the Virginia plan's scheme of proportional representation, Paterson proposed equal representation for all states. His oratorical and legal skills made it eminently clear that the continued large-state insistence on proportional representation would thoroughly undermine the convention. The Connecticut compromise, giving equal representation in the Senate and proportional representation in the House of Representatives, saved the convention.

Paterson was elected one of New Jersey's first senators in March 1789 and served as governor of the state from 1790 to 1793. In 1793 he was appointed associate justice of the United States Supreme Court; he served until his death in 1806.

Loyalists

Between 1777 and 1781 the legislature, following the lead of the East Jersey delegates, passed a number of bills in support of the war effort, including a number of antiloyalist measures. On the whole there was little serious disagreement over the treatment of the loyalists. In 1777 the legislature required all voters to take an oath of allegiance to the state and barred from office any person who had aided the enemy. In the same year it made the estates of those who had joined the British subject to forfeiture. By the end of 1778 the legislature established procedures for the identification of loyalists and the confiscation and sale of their estates. Confiscation of loyalist property was widely supported in principle, though there was some disagreement about what kind of loyalist should have his property confiscated. Between 1778 and 1789 New Jersey confiscated and sold at least five hundred loyalist estates, realizing about £1,507,300 for the state treasury. While the war was still in progress the depreciation of the value of the paper money taken in payment dramatically reduced this economic windfall in real terms, and in June 1781 sales were temporarily suspended in recognition of the diminishing returns. On the whole, active loyalists were the ones most seriously affected by the policy of confiscation. Those who had fought or fled behind British lines were not welcomed back to New Jersey after the war. Many moderate loyalists or neutrals, depending on where they lived, successfully waited out much of the animosity and retained their property.

The end of the war revived the question of what to do with the confiscated property. The provisions of the Treaty of Paris which called for Congress to recommend the restoration of loyalist rights and property were not popular, either with those who had purchased the properties or with those who had suffered at the hands of the loyalists. Congress duly recommended; the states ignored the recommendation. Public pressure to resume sales stimulated the legislature to authorize additional sales beginning in December 1783. In addition, all those who had fled to British lines, been adjudged guilty of treason, refused to take the oath of allegiance or had their property confiscated were barred from holding any state office or voting in state elections. In August 1784 the sales were suspended for two years after evidence of fraud had surfaced. The political rights of Loyalists were restored in 1788. In 1789 the sale of confiscated estates came to an end, but confiscated property was not returned.

In 1783 and 1784 there were some halfhearted attempts to encourage loyalists to return. In May 1783 John Rutherfurd, a member of a wealthy family of merchants and landowners, suggested in a letter to an unidentified New Jersey legislator that wealthy loyalist merchants should be invited to move to New Jersey and use their wealth to advance the state's commercial position. A firm believer in the principle that "Merchants thrive by Merchants," Rutherfurd painted a rosy picture of the benefits to be derived from the successful enticement of loyalist merchants.

> For it is past a Doubt that such a Capital in such Useful Hands would give a new Complection to the whole State; ... give Employment to our Youth now languishing in Idleness; raise the Rents of our Lands and Houses, and consequently raise their Value; lower the Prices of Goods; furnish Sums to Borrowers without going out of the State; make Money plentier; and make both the Farmer and Mechanick better able to pay their Taxes, which is a thing we should principally have in View.[8]

Rutherfurd's motives were not entirely innocent. He had been a neutral during the war, and his chief supporters in this plan were his father, Walter Rutherfurd, and James

Parker. Both Rutherford and Parker had major landholdings, and both had been fined and imprisoned during the war for refusing to take the oath of allegiance. Parker later became the agent for Sir Robert Barker, an Englishman with substantial landholdings whose tenants refused to recognize his right to collect their rents.

Nothing came of Rutherfurd's proposal until the following spring when a series of letters appeared in the New Brunswick paper, the *Political Intelligencer,* promoting a similar scheme. In August 1784 a number of East Jersey merchants circulated a proposal, later adopted by the legislature, calling for the establishment of free ports in Perth Amboy and Burlington. Citizenship would be granted to any merchant who resided in either city for one month, except persons "guilty of licentious Cruelties in Plundering or Murder."[9] The group hoped to attract loyalist or neutralist merchants who had been hounded out of other states. The measure as passed by the legislature also exempted foreign goods from duties and the merchants' stock and possessions from taxation. The legislature's acquiescence in this plan was as much a desire to increase trade at the expense of Philadelphia and New York as it was a move to reintegrate loyalists into society. Very little came of it. However, the proposal does indicate a surprising lack of hostility towards loyalists in a state with a history of violent patriot-loyalist conflict.

The success of the restrictions on loyalists varied widely, but many left New Jersey during and after the war. Some of those who left had held positions of importance in government or business or had been leaders in society. Their departure disrupted the social, economic and political fabric of New Jersey, but it also provided an opportunity for new men to rise to influence.

The Dividing Line Controversy

A sharp dispute about the proper boundary dividing East and West Jersey claimed the attention of both sets of proprietors in the first years after the war. The exact location of the northern point of the line had remained uncertain from the beginnings of settlement. The line established by John Lawrence in 1743 at the behest of the East Jersey proprietors was not accepted by the West Jersey group. In 1769 a royal commission established the boundary between New Jersey and New York. The commission set the North Station Point (the northern point of the line separating East from West Jersey) several miles east of the location Lawrence had marked. The marking granted the West Jersey proprietors a windfall of several hundred thousand acres of valuable land (see figure 2). A good deal of the land was saleable at a handsome profit. Keen to retain this benefit, the West Jersey proprietors sought to have the Provincial Assembly confirm the dividing line. The East Jersey proprietors, not surprisingly, resisted. The war postponed legal action, although West Jersey continued its attempts to survey the area.

The war's end brought a renewal of the dispute. Both boards of proprietors dispatched lawyers to Trenton to argue their respective cases before the legislature. In 1784 the East Jersey proprietors won a close legislative vote, seventeen to sixteen. Encouraged by the slimness of the majority, the West Jersey proprietors renewed their efforts, but it was for naught. In 1786 East Jersey again won: this time the margin was considerably larger, twenty-three to thirteen. The West Jersey proprietors then repaired to the courts, attempting to eject landowners whose titles depended on East Jersey surveys in the disputed territory. Eventually the prospect of a series of

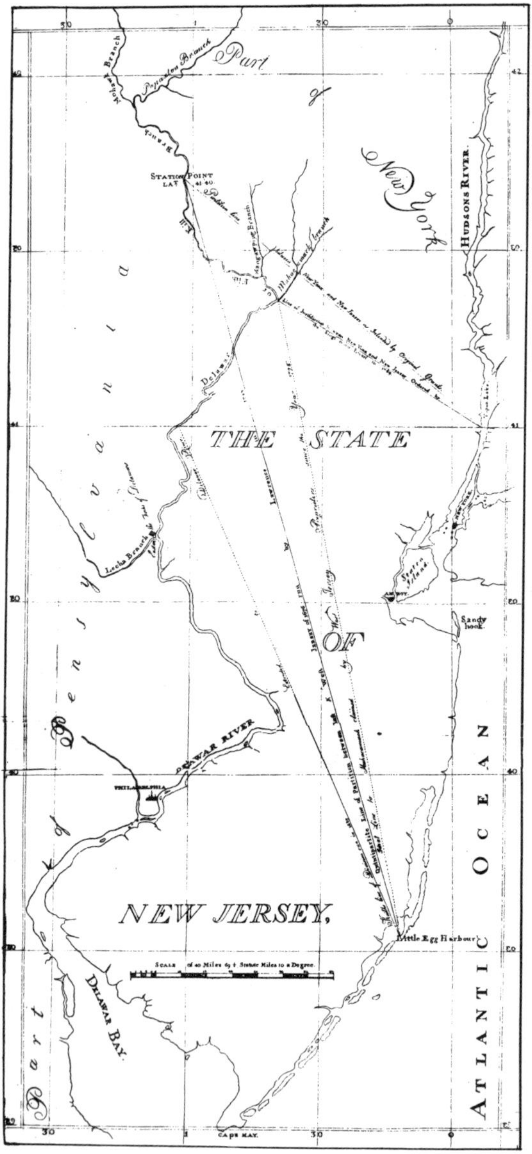

THE STATE
OF
NEW JERSEY,
ATLANTIC OCEAN
HUDSONS RIVER
DELAWAR RIVER
DELAWAR BAY
PHILADELPHIA
Little Egg Harbour
Sandy hook.
Staten Island
STATION POINT
CAPE MAY
Part of New York
Part of Pensylvania

inconclusive and highly expensive lawsuits made common sense prevail, and the controversy subsided.

The dispute was important in its own right because the land was quite valuable. However, the controversy's effect on postwar politics was more significant. In the postwar period, the two groups of proprietors might have combined to temper the influence of the agrarian debtors. Instead, they spent the years from 1782 to 1786 in hot dispute, intent on achieving a favorable ruling from the legislature. The East Jersey proprietors, loath to offend their own legislators, mounted no opposition to the paper money and prodebtor measures their representatives were supporting. Ordinarily the East and West Jersey proprietors would have formed a united conservative front and made common cause with the creditors. They did not, and the New Jersey legislature passed a considerable body of prodebtor legislation in the 1780s.

Rascals and Artful Designing Men

The economic depression of the mid-1780s had a devastating impact on many of New Jersey's citizens, particularly the merchants, farmers and small manufacturers. The largest and most vocal group was the farmers. As the number of lawsuits

Figure 2. *Boundary Lines Separating East from West Jersey, Surveyed Between 1676 and 1775. From William H. Shaw, comp.*, History of Essex and Hudson Counties, New Jersey *(1884).*

The Keith Line (left) was drawn in 1687; the Quintipartite Line (middle) was drawn in 1676 and extended as the Lawrence Line in 1743; and the line claimed by the West Jersey proprietors (right) was drawn in 1775. The dispute between the West and East Jersey proprietors concerned the land between the Lawrence Line and the line of 1775.

for recovery of debt grew, public pressure for a paper-money bill increased.

The two contrasting models available to New Jersey for dealing with its economic problems were Massachusetts and Rhode Island. Massachusetts followed an absolute procreditor, hard-money line and eventually paid for it with armed agrarian unrest. Rhode Island followed an extreme prodebtor, soft-money policy which made it illegal for creditors to refuse to accept payment in Rhode Island currency. As a result, creditors fled the state to avoid payment in paper currency. New Jersey had advocates of both courses. The state leaned towards one approach or the other during the 1780s, depending upon which group controlled the legislature. On the whole, the legislature adopted a middle course.

Paper money had been a successful form of finance in specie-poor New Jersey and in other colonies for much of the eighteenth century. Since specie (gold or silver) was paid to exporting countries in exchange for goods like textiles, books or wine, the importing colonies often faced a shortage of a circulating medium of exchange. Currency finance was a convenient solution to this problem. In broad terms, it took one of two forms. A colonial government issued paper money or certificates, paid its debts with them and took them back in the form of taxes. Or the government established a land bank which issued paper money and lent it at interest to borrowers, who used their land as collateral. When the loans were repaid, the principal was withdrawn from circulation and destroyed and the interest supported government expenses. The loan office had a successful history in New Jersey. New Jersey's management of its loan offices had been conservative, and New Jersey money had kept its value fairly well. It had even, at various times, been a desired medium of exchange in neighboring colonies.

The Crown was skeptical of paper money and consistently opposed it as legal tender. Colonial paper money did tend

Postwar Dilemmas and Controversies

to depreciate, and in some colonies it was very unstable. British merchants, unenthusiastic about a decline in their margin of profit, did not like to accept it in payment for goods.

In the 1780s debtors favored paper money for much the same reasons as before the war. Specie was scarce and money did not circulate widely in the stagnant economy of the postwar period. In consequence, people found it difficult to pay either their debts or their taxes. Creditors, on the other hand, opposed paper money for reasons similar to those cited by the Crown and British merchants. The paper money issued during the war had depreciated wildly. When creditors were repaid in depreciated currency they received less than their due.

East Jersey was an area of many creditors as well as debtors. The major spokesmen on both sides of the paper money dispute were all East Jersey men. Abraham Clark was the chief exponent of soft or paper money and other measures for debtor relief; William Livingston and William Paterson were strong supporters of the procreditor, hard-money position. Because East Jersey had far more debtors than creditors, most of its representatives tended to support prodebtor measures, including any soft- or paper-money proposals as well as specific bills for debtor relief. Payments on the state and Continental debt represented most of the expenses of government. During the war East Jersey representatives, most of whom were men of moderate means, had generally supported governmental expenditures. As the war ended, their willingness to spend money diminished. Because taxes had to be paid in specie, which was scarce, they voted against measures which required an increase in taxes. These measures included bills raising the salaries of government officials and bills providing for debt payments. It was a situation fraught with irony. East Jerseyans held most of the debt and needed the interest payments, but with specie scarce their representatives opposed raising the money to meet the payments. Once they gained control of the legislature in 1785 and could pursue an ultimately successful campaign for a paper money bill, their opposition to money measures lessened.

West Jersey legislators as a group included more men of wealth. West Jersey was not as specie-poor as the rest of the state and could have supplied the specie for debt payments. During the war West Jersey legislators had opposed money measures in support of armed conflict. When the war ended they were more inclined to vote for money bills to support government expenditures—unless those measures were in support of debt payments.

The legislature passed a number of prodebtor measures in 1781–1786. The legislation included bills forcing creditors to accept paper money, penalizing creditors who had refused paper money in the past, releasing debtors from confinement, delaying court proceedings in debt cases and reducing their cost, and preventing the forced sale of debtor estates at reduced value. Creditors were dismayed. In their eyes, the debtor relief measures were dangerous because they violated the sanctity of contracts and damaged public and private credit.

The law preventing the sale of debtor estates at reduced value, sometimes called the "Bull Law," was the product of Abraham Clark's fertile mind. Debtors had seen their property sold at public auction for a fraction of the actual value. Clark's law forced creditors to accept enough property at appraised value to satisfy the debt. An analysis of the assembly's vote on this measure in March 1786 shows that 87 percent of the West Jersey delegates took a procreditor position opposing the bill, as compared to only 24 percent of the East Jersey delegates. Many assemblymen from the northern counties of West Jersey, however, voted with East Jersey, as they often did on money matters during the postwar period. Only one-third of the Sussex County delegation opposed the bill, and none of the Hunterdon County delegates did. The law was repealed in November following a storm of criticism.

William Paterson was firmly of the opinion that "citizens should be faithful and punctual in the Performance of Contracts and Payment of Debts" and that the legislature "should leave the parties to the law under which they contracted."[10] The major portion of Paterson's thriving legal practice involved debt cases, and he represented the creditor in nearly all of them. He particularly disliked the Bull Law and had little use for what he saw as the legislature's cowardice:

> the Legislature must have been sensible of the injustice and terpitude of the measure; but they supposed it would have been pleasing to the bulk of their constituents, and therefore suffered themselves to be carried away by what they conceived to be a popular current.[11]

The October 1785 legislative session convened in the midst of public pressure for additional debtor relief. Despite the public clamor, the assembly did not vote on the loan-office measure. It referred it to a committee which would report at the February 1786 session.

The passage of the loan-office bill was the major achievement of this session. Between December 1785 and April 1786 a lively debate erupted over the merits of paper money, featuring Clark, Livingston and Paterson. Writing under the pseudonyms "Willing to Learn" and "Primitive Whig," Clark and Livingston argued the case in a series of strongly worded newspaper articles. Clark's entire argument also appeared the same year in an anonymous pamphlet, *The True Policy of New-Jersey, Defined.*

Paterson and Livingston attributed the reluctance to pay taxes to a lack of moral fiber rather than an inability to pay. Both argued that there was no scarcity of money. Borrowing cash was difficult simply because creditors believed the legislature would once more undercut their investments with anticreditor legislation. Livingston scornfully described a "lazy, lounging, lubberly fellow sitting nights and days in a tippling house" who seldom worked and was overpaid when he did. This fellow squandered his money in "riot and debauch" and then complained at tax time "of the hardness of the times, and the want of a circulating medium." His pen well dipped in vitriol, Livingston asked,

> But who is that yonder honest looking farmer, who shakes his head at the name of taxes, and protests that he cannot pay them! Why, he is a man whose three daughters are under the discipline of a French dancing-master, when they ought every one of them to be at the spinning-wheel; and who, while they should be dressed in decent homespun, as were their frugal grand-mothers, now carry half of their father's crop upon their backs.[12]

Paterson shared Livingston's belief that people were not destitute but dissolute, spending their money on foreign luxuries. He wrote indignantly,

> The indolent and dissipated may clamour about the Scarcity of Money; the one will not toil to get it, & the other squanders it as fast as he receives: their clamour would be the same, if they possessed all the mines of Peru.[13]

Clark, who called himself "A Fellow Citizen" in his pamphlet, celebrated the farmer and the mechanic as the bulwark of the state and the reason for its progress. The pamphlet described high taxes as a universal hardship. Taxes on one item would "not only enhance the price of that particular article, but [would have] influence in raising the price of all husbandry and manufacturers." He observed drily, "we are so much afraid that the inhabitants of New-Jersey will be industrious, that we will tax them even for making the attempt." For Clark, the scarcity of money was a calamity, one made worse by greed.

> It is now next to an impossibility for an honest man, who can give good security, to procure money on interest; and many such we

see, by misfortune or otherwise, owe money which it is not now in their power to pay, many of whom are obliged to submit to prosecutions, and to have their estates sold far below the value, to the breaking of families and increase of poverty.... Those who have horded the hard money, or have large sums due them from individuals, are many of them expecting greatly to increase their fortunes by the general calamity, and who but they have caused the distress.[14]

He warned that the scarcity of money was "promoting that inequality of property which is detrimental in a republican government."[15]

Livingston asserted that paper money was desired only because the debtors, "idle spendthrifts" and "dissipating drones of the community" wanted to cheat their creditors out of what was rightfully due them. He looked forward to the day "when laws [would] be made in favour of creditors instead of debtors; and when no cozening, trickish, fraudulent scoundrel [should] be able to plead legal protection for his cozenage, tricks, frauds and rascality."[16]

Both sides were convinced of the morality and fiscal responsibility of their respective positions. Livingston acknowledged that self-interest prompted the creditors' position on the loan-office bill, just as it did the debtors'. However, he claimed that the creditor's interest coincided with the community's. The creditor sought to restore national credit by opposing the issue of paper money that was sure to depreciate. The debtor sought to evade his responsibility to pay his debt. Clark argued that creditors and speculators sought to reap extraordinary profit from the misfortunes of others. Livingston insisted that paper money inevitably depreciated. Clark pointed out that there would be no incentive for the state, which would issue the paper money, to depreciate its value. The state as creditor would hardly reduce the value of its investment.

Livingston argued that the prospect of further loan-office money discouraged the settlement of foreigners. He painted a picture of thousands of Europeans, "gentlemen of middling fortunes," who would prefer the political freedom and lower taxes of America. America presented admirable investment opportunities, but these gentlemen would not chance investment where there was "no security for property, no stability in publick bodies as to the redemption of paper currency emitted upon the most solemn assurances."[17] Clark argued that whatever hard money was invested would shortly leave New Jersey in payment for foreign trade; the state would have no circulating money. New Jersey must have paper money, and it must be legal tender in all cases lest it depreciate. The idea of encouraging tories to return to New Jersey and invest triggered a vigorous response from Clark. Tories were "pests and traitors to New-Jersey." New Jerseyans should not permit them "to dwell among us because they have money; should we not rather spurn them from us as filth, and not take those adders in our bosom merely for the love of money."[18]

Both sides were scathing in their denunciations of their opponents. In his last essay, Livingston used the fiction of a letter from Martha Hardlines, a "venerable and distressed widow." The imaginary Ms. Hardlines, paid in depreciated money by her debtors, "those hardened wretches," described herself as "from ease and plenty ... reduced ... to the drudgery of a scullion." Livingston concluded his essay with a query from the infirm daughter with whom he had equipped his fictional widow: *"Pray, mama, will there never be an end of this paper currency that seems contrived to ruin poor widows and orphans like you and me?"*[19]

Paterson called for a decrease in the amount of currency available. He identified luxury with corruption and frugality with virtue. Republican government would not survive in an atmosphere of corruption.

> It must be the Wish of every good Man, as it is in the interest of every wise man, that Money should decrease and not increase among

us. A decrease of Money will introduce a Spirit of Industry & Frugality, will restrain luxury, Extravagance and thoughtless Profusion, and will compel people to work for the Bread they eat, and not go about seeking whom they may devour.[20]

Clark depicted his opponents as "artful, designing men" and warned about their campaign against the loan office.

And the moneyed-men not yet satisfied, are pressing the matter farther and wishing for greater power to grind the face of the needy ... and not be under the necessity of getting their bread by industry, but may live by the labour of the honest farmer and mechanic ... living in idleness by other mens toil....

BEWARE, my countrymen of New-Jersey ... BEWARE: Lest although we have knocked off the shackles of British tyranny we should suffer ourselves to be duped into as bad a situation by artful interested designing men....

Behold! Artful designing men of different classes, each setting on foot (and sending to the different counties to obtain signers) petitions to our legislature which have a tendancy, if granted, not to promote the general good of the state, but their avaricious thirst for gain.[21]

There was strong public support for the loan-office bill in all counties except Bergen, Cumberland and Cape May. However, the overwhelming majority of legislators from southern New Jersey opposed it—generally on the grounds that the legislators would not be faithful to any promise to maintain the value of the money. Two votes (November 25, 1785, and March 9, 1786) on the paper money measure show a pattern similar to that described for the Bull Law. On the first vote 39 percent of East Jersey delegates and 77 percent of West Jersey delegates opposed the measure. On the second, the percentages opposing were 24 percent for East Jersey and 87 percent for West Jersey.

The paper-money measure finally passed in May 1786. Because borrowers had to furnish land as security, the loan-office act did little to ease the situation of those without land.

Postwar Dilemmas and Controversies

However, the debate over the money question subsided fairly quickly. Perhaps the assembly's sensitivity to the problems of debtors helped New Jersey avoid the kind of agrarian unrest that afflicted Massachusetts.

4

New Jersey in the New Nation

During the state's attempts to address the problem of its debtors and creditors, Congress's currency crisis remained unresolved. For most of the period until late 1779 Congress simply issued paper money. After the Articles were ratified, Congress requisitioned money from the states, establishing a system that was less inflationary but unequal to the financial requirements of government. The weight of private debt made the problem of public debt more urgent. With no revenue from ports or western lands, New Jersey could meet Congress's requisitions only by taxing its citizens, many of whom were the same Continental creditors Congress was attempting to satisfy. Not surprisingly, New Jersey was a strong advocate of alternative means to support the government.

Not Worth A Continental

In March 1780 the Continental Congress concluded that the system of paper credit which it had used to finance the war required major and immediate reorganization. Throughout the war the states and the Continental Congress had issued several forms of paper money to support the army. The money had fallen in value until October 1780, when $77.50 in Continental currency bought only $1.00 in specie. While few men in the Continental Congress were ignorant of the possible dangers of a depreciating currency, there had been little alternative to paper money as a means of financing the Revolution.

Congress had issued $6 million in 1775, the first year of its new Continental currency. As the money declined in value, Congress printed more. Except for a brief period in 1778, when news of the French alliance bolstered the value of Continental currency, it depreciated steadily. By independence, Congress had issued more than $25 million; by 1779 the total had reached $263 million, most of which remained in circulation. Total federal income for the period 1777 through 1780 has been estimated at $55.3 million (specie value), of which $45.5 million was in Continental currency. The cost of the war was staggering. Though difficult to estimate with accuracy, Congress may have spent $85 million (specie) through 1781, or about $12 million a year.

Money issued by individual states and paper certificates or promises to pay given by state and Continental purchasing agents added to the sea of paper. This paper was worth little more than a fraction of its face value.

By late 1779 Congress was so poverty-stricken that it resorted to requisitioning commodities to supply the army, commodities it could not afford to purchase with its rapidly depreciating currency. The winter of 1779–80, when Washington was encamped at Morristown, was the worst of the war. Congress could neither pay the army nor supply it. Merchants and farmers refused to provide food or any other necessities. In May 1780, Connecticut regiments mutinied briefly, demanding full rations and five months' back pay. The following winter there were more serious incidents, again over shortages of food and arrearages of pay. On January 1, 1781 the Pennsylvania line, exasperated and claiming that their terms of enlistment had expired, left their Morristown camp and marched, armed, towards Philadelphia to demand a redress of grievances from their own state officials. The mutiny was touched off when recruiting agents appeared, willing to pay new enlistees a bounty of hard coin. Within several days negotiations ended the mutiny, and the discharged soldiers reenlisted for the bounty. On January 20 some portions of the New Jersey line, sympathetic to the Pennsylvanians and emboldened by their success, mutinied at Pompton. They were quickly brought under control, and two of their number were executed.

In 1780 an impoverished Congress asked the states to assume the burden of paying for their own Continental soldiers. Most states complied and compensated their soldiers for periods of service into 1782 as well as for losses due to the depreciating currency. The military or depreciation certificates the states issued were a substantial burden and represented the bulk of the state debts in the postwar period.

In March 1780 Congress decided to call in its old paper money. However, it overvalued the old currency in relation to specie. In essence it repudiated its old currency, reducing the legal value of the debt to one-fortieth of what it had been. Under the plan the states were to take the old currency when taxes were collected and then deliver it to Congress, which would destroy it. New currency would be issued, based on the credit of the individual states and at a proportion of $1 to every $20 turned in. The delivering state would receive 60 percent of the new currency, and Congress would receive 40 percent. The new money, legal tender, was to be redeemed by each state over a period of six years.

New Jersey's quota was $11,700,000. Collecting the entire amount would entitle the state to $600,000 in the new currency. The state embraced the new system, and the legislature passed the necessary tax law. As the old money came in, the state duly deposited it in the Continental loan office. New Jersey was flooded with a variety of paper certificates, but the amount of Continental currency circulating fell well short of the quota. The state collected less than $7 million and was alloted about $336,000 in the new currency. Since a portion of the new currency was never issued, $7 million in Continental currency was actually replaced by $291,000 in state money.

Many merchants and a significant number of inhabitants of West Jersey had little faith in the new currency and refused to accept it. It depreciated quickly, principally because the value of the old currency in relation to specie had been set too high. The legislature attempted to maintain the value of the new currency, but no law could make the currency equal to specie.

A controversy over the new currency's value developed largely along sectional lines. On one side were West Jersey legislators. West Jersey, which had not suffered much of the war's conflict or received much of the paper money which financed the struggle, had little of the new currency. Its representatives wanted the money redeemed at current value, the lowest cost to their region. Representatives of a varied group of East Jerseyans took the other side. Fiscal conservatives and the public creditors, a group largely based in East Jersey and one which included a number of speculators, viewed repudiation as a faithless breach of contract. They wanted redemption at face value.

The legislature made several attempts to deal with the knotty problem of redemption. On each occasion sectional divisions in the legislature thwarted the effort. In the fall of 1782 a new tax was required to retire the next scheduled installment. The necessary bill provided for redemption at par; all of the West Jersey assembly members combined with four East Jersey members to defeat it. After this defeat the assembly directed the state treasurer to issue no additional money until the remaining $122,000 was retired. The legislative stalemate continued through a special session in May 1783 and regular sessions in December 1783 and August 1784. The assembly agreed on redemption at depreciated value at both regular sessions, but the council rejected the measure. The October 1784 elections changed the makeup of the council. Assembly and council finally agreed on a tax redeeming the new currency issue at the depreciated value of 3 to 1 of specie. Legislators from Middlesex, Monmouth and Somerset sided with those from West Jersey. Presumably the East Jersey legislators who voted for repudiation believed both that redemption of depreciated currency at face value would unfairly benefit an unpopular minority and that the depreciated value was better than nothing.

Western Lands

New Jersey's problems with the Confederation extended beyond the currency issue. Many states were disturbed by the absence of any provision in the Articles of Confederation for the disposition of lands formerly held by the British Crown. New Jersey and other states without claims to western lands, wanting to limit the claims of states like Virginia, argued that these former Crown lands belonged in common to the union. The land question became a major roadblock to final ratification of the Articles. Maryland did not ratify the Articles until February 1781 because of the uncertainty surrounding the disposition of the western lands. At issue were the competing claims of seven states—Virginia, New York, Connecticut, Massachusetts, North Carolina, South Carolina and Georgia—and several land companies to a vast stretch of territory extending west to the Mississippi River (see figure 3). All in all, the claims amounted to about 150 million acres.

New Jersey's attitude was prompted both by its precarious economic situation and by the presence in the legislature of men who had invested in speculative land companies. The land companies based their claims on Indian deeds they had

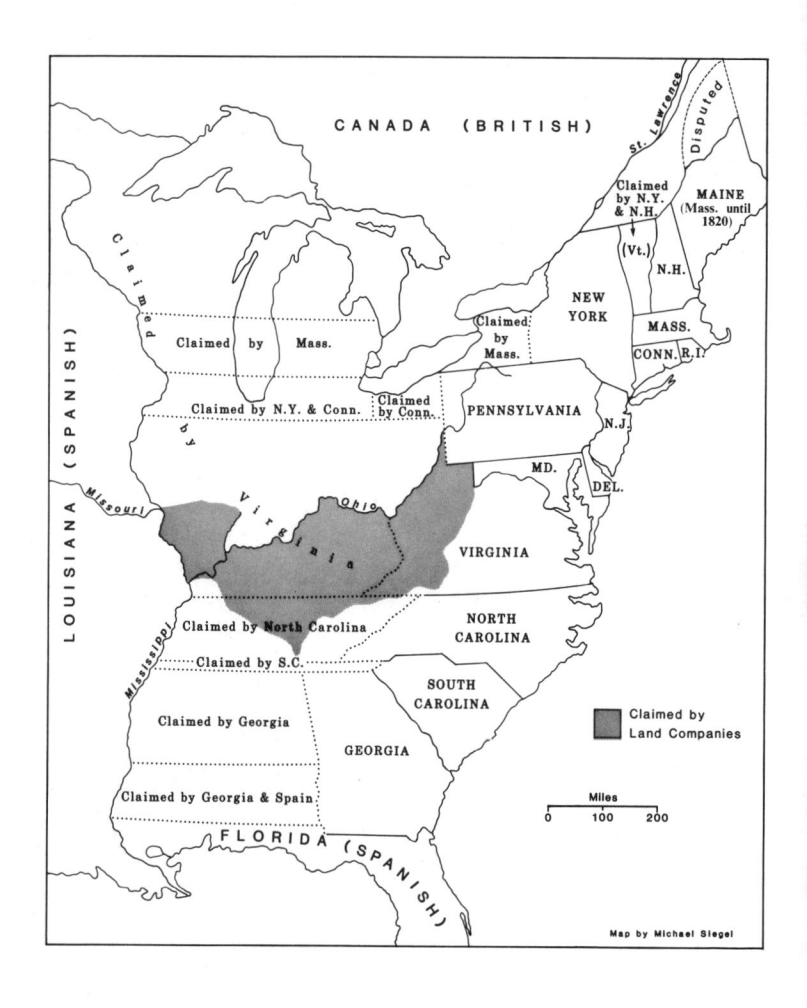

Figure 3. *The United States in the Confederation Period: The Thirteen States and the Western Lands Claimed by the States and the Land Companies. Map by Michael Siegel, Center for Coastal and Environmental Studies, Rutgers University.*

purchased. However, many of the states, citing their original charters, claimed the same lands. They wanted to retain their territory, or at least have the claims of the land companies negated before ceding any territory to the nation.

New Jersey was particularly opposed to Virginia's rather extravagant claim to the vast tracts of land north and south of the Ohio River. The contention that Congress should simply assert its own claim at the expense of those of the individual states was unreasonable. The Articles offered no method of settling issues between one state and the Confederation as a whole, and they certainly provided no means of compelling a state to give away its territory. Moreover, Congress's sporadic attempts to adjudicate between states proved unwise. The eventual solution—a series of cessions by the states that claimed the lands—was tedious but avoided the difficult problem of sovereignty.

In 1780 Virginia opened a land office in the territory south of the Ohio River and requested that Congress confirm its grants. Congress recommended that the states cede portions of their claims. The New Jersey assembly appointed a committee to investigate its citizens' complaints about the western claims. The Indiana Company, which counted many prominent citizens of New Jersey among its investors, was represented on the committee. Not surprisingly, the committee's report concluded that the lands belonged to the states in common. In December 1780 the assembly sent Congress a memorial based on the report.

In January 1781 Virginia offered Congress a bargain. It would cede the entire northern portion of its western claim—if all prior Indian claims were voided and its rights to the remaining territory south of the Ohio River were confirmed. New Jersey, among other states, objected strenuously. In October 1781 the New Jersey assembly instructed its delegates to the Congress to oppose the cession and demand a resolution of the Indiana Company claims. In

November Congress rejected Virginia's proposal. The issue remained unresolved until March 1784, when Congress accepted the partial cession in a compromise. The compromise incorporated an understanding that the Indian grants would not be upheld, but it omitted any mention of territorial guarantees.

Dissatisfied with the proposed compromise, New Jersey attempted to bring the land dispute before the Confederation as a suit between the states of Virginia and New Jersey. When this failed New Jersey voted against the Virginia land cession. As late as March 1784, long after the land question had been resolved, New Jersey's legislature continued to instruct its delegates to oppose any western lands bill if the legislation might benefit one state exclusively.

New Jersey considered the western lands to be important, both as a source of revenue for the central government and as a prime area where the state's many impoverished farmers might seek a new start. However, the opening of the West to settlement depended upon the free navigation of the Mississippi River, and New Jersey's position on this issue differed from that of other northern states.

In the Treaty of Paris Britain had conceded the right to free navigation of the Mississippi, but Spain actually controlled the region. Spain was in general displeased that the treaty had set the Mississippi River, rather than the Appalachian Divide, as the western boundary of the United States. To protect their territory, the Spanish closed the river to American shipping. Further, they demanded the renunciation of any American claim to free navigation of the Mississippi as the price of a commercial treaty.

Most of the northern states were quite willing to give up free navigation for a commercial treaty with Spain. A treaty would provide commercial opportunities for eastern cities hard pressed by the postwar economic depression and give some commercial standing to the new nation. Continued closure of the Mississippi River would prevent the expansion of the West, an area that all regions expected the South to dominate. Containing the West would keep southern influence in the Confederation in check.

The South promoted the opening of the West, not only because expansion would increase its influence, but because the South feared the West might opt for independence if it were not brought into the Confederation quickly.

Negotiations between Spain and the United States began in 1785. The Spanish chargé d'affaires, Diego de Gardoqui, was affable but adamant. John Jay, a New Yorker and the American negotiator, concluded that an insistence on free navigation was futile and requested a change in his instructions. In August 1786 Congress agreed to revise the instructions. Initially, two of New Jersey's three delegates supported revision. But Virginia, convinced that New Jersey might be persuaded that the opening of the West to settlement was more important than a treaty with Spain, directed James Madison to approach Abraham Clark at the Annapolis Convention that had been called to discuss matters of trade (see page 66).

Though Clark was not a congressional delegate, he was an important figure in the state legislature. After meeting with Madison he persuaded the legislature to instruct the state's congressional delegates to return to the old position.

A commercial treaty with Spain was attractive to those northern states blessed with ports and shipping industries. It was of little interest to New Jersey, which had neither. The value of the western lands depended on opening the area for settlement. Once Congress controlled the western lands, New Jersey favored any course that increased their value.

Popular opposition to Jay and to the renunciation of a claim to free navigation increased. Negotiations with the Spanish ground to a halt and were only resumed later under the Constitution.

The Movable Capital

New Jersey was one of several states to offer a permanent site for the national capital during the 1780s. Between 1776 and 1784 Congress met in many different locations. It fled Philadelphia, its first site, twice in the 1770s in response to British military threats. In 1783 it left Philadelphia again, this time moving to Princeton to evade an angry contingent of the Continental army demanding back pay.

New Jersey's attempts to secure the federal capital ran afoul of both sectional rivalries and a struggle between those who favored a strong national government and those who did not. Philadelphia made many delegates nervous. It was not the rural setting that republican ideology associated with virtue; rather, it was the center of power of a group, led by Superintendent of Finance Robert Morris, that worked unceasingly to strengthen the power of the national government. Some southern delegates supported the idea of a strong national government but favored a southern capital. A group of eastern and southern delegates who were opposed to a strong national government could agree only that the capital should not be in Philadelphia. Offers of permanent sites abounded in 1783, including overtures from Annapolis, Georgetown, Kingston (New York), and five locations in New Jersey (Trenton, Nottingham [now Trenton and Hamilton], Newark, New Brunswick and Elizabethtown). Congress had little more success deciding on a temporary site—Annapolis, New York, Princeton and Philadelphia were all considered.

Once Philadelphia had been rejected, two sites emerged as the most likely choices—one near the falls of the Potomac, the other near the falls of the Delaware. Both were centrally located on navigable bodies of water, and neither was near a large city and its associated corruption. New England and the middle states supported the Delaware falls site; the South voted for the Potomac. Outvoted, the South threatened to press for a Philadelphia site and to block any construction funds for a Delaware falls site. A coalition of eastern and southern delegates capitalized on the temporary absence of delegates from Pennsylvania, New Jersey and Delaware and passed a resolution calling for two sites. The permanent capital would alternate between sites on the falls of the Delaware and the falls of the Potomac. Trenton and Annapolis would be the alternate sites of the temporary capital. Exasperated, New Jerseyan Elias Boudinot, the president of the Congress, wrote to Robert Morris,

> You have undoubtedly heard of the late maneuvers relating to our erratic residence. It gives me real distress, as I fear it is laying a solid Foundation for future divisions. It was not obtained in the most candid and generous way, and was finally accomplished by the most heterogenous Coalition that was in the power of Congress to Form.[22]

The secretary of Congress, Charles Thomson, sent his wife Hannah an indignant report of the maneuvers on October 17, 1783.

> I think I mentioned in a former letter that in order to engage the Southern States not to vote for a temporary residence in Philadelphia the eastern members had it in contemplation to propose two places for erecting buildings for the residence of Congress.... If the public treasury was full of money or if the public debts were paid, or funds provided for discharging them or even for the regular payment of the interest, one might hear such projects with patience. But in the present state of affairs to talk of building cities, when they can scarcely furnish money to buy paper on which to draw a plan of them .... appears to me something different from wisdom, prudence or policy.[23]

The poet Francis Hopkinson suggested sarcastically that Congress either build a wooden equestrian statue of George Washington large enough to contain all the members of

Congress and float it from one capital to another, or equip every government building with giant sails and bellows for their convenient transport between the capitals.

The dual capital proposal did not survive very long. In October 1784 Congress again voted for a Delaware falls site and designated New York as the temporary capital. Victory seemed within New Jersey's grasp, but lack of money prevented any building construction. Though the South eventually prevailed, a New Jersey site for the federal capital was still a possibility when the state considered the Constitution. The vision of a federal capital in New Jersey may well have contributed to the state's enthusiasm for the new frame of government.

Impost

Congress desperately needed a source of revenue. In November 1780 it considered several proposals to secure itself an independent income and settled on an import tax or impost as the most promising. In February 1781, before ratification of the Articles was complete, Congress asked the states to amend the document and give Congress the authority to levy a 5 percent tax on certain imports—a move New Jersey favored heartily. Twelve states approved the 1781 impost, but passage required the assent of all thirteen. Rhode Island, protecting its own revenue activities, rejected the impost in November 1782.

In September 1782 Congress made an emergency requisition on the states to pay the interest on the debt. New Jersey's legislature took no action on the requisition, an oversight which irritated the state's many Continental creditors. Stung by their criticism, the legislature passed the required legislation in June 1783. In December the legislature moved to protect these creditors and bypass the requisition system it considered inequitable. It instructed the state treasurer to pay the money directly to local creditors.

Meanwhile, Congress was again at work on a scheme to secure itself a regular income. In April 1783 it asked the states for the authority to levy a 5 percent import tax on certain goods for a period of twenty-five years. The proceeds would be used for debt payments. In addition, it requested a supplemental revenue, also for twenty-five years, and the cession of all former Crown lands still held by the states.

The New Jersey legislature had little reason to believe that all thirteen states would agree to this impost when they had not approved the previous one. Nevertheless, the legislature approved the impost and the land cession but it delayed action on the supplemental revenue. In December 1783 the legislature approved a bill imposing the necessary tax for the next twenty-five years. Because specie was scarce, it made the tax payable in paper money and ordered the printing of an amount equal to New Jersey's quota of the supplemental revenue. But, as it had done with the emergency requisition, it ordered the state treasurer to pay local creditors directly rather than forwarding any money to the Confederation treasury. In December 1784 the legislature reaffirmed its decision and ordered the state treasurer to make no further payment on Congress's requisitions until the states approved the impost.

5

Toward a New Nation

Confrontation

As expected, all thirteen states did not approve the financial plan. New Jersey's failure to meet the requisition had no immediate impact because Congress issued no new call for funds until September 1785. The September requisition was couched in language which exasperated New Jersey's legislators. Congress announced it would not be responsible for interest payments that any state made to its own Continental creditors after January 1786. Further, it refused to issue interest certificates to any public creditor residing in a state which failed to comply with the requisition.

The legislature fumed. New Jersey had expected to be reimbursed at some future point for the payments made to Continental creditors. In a December 9 letter to the state's congressional delegation, assemblyman Abraham Clark pointed out that New Jersey had incurred considerable expense by shouldering Congress's financial burden. The state had arranged to compensate Continental creditors before state creditors. Why should it now be penalized for doing so? Moreover, New Jersey's citizens had lent money to Congress as private citizens. No action of the legislature of the state where they resided should interfere with repayment. Supply-

Toward a New Nation

ing New Jersey's share of the requisition required oppressive taxes, and its citizens also paid imposts to New York and Pennsylvania, contributing handsomely to *their* share of the requisition. Clark described the requisition as a

> Scheme ... by some intended to give a final Stab to the impost, tho' not long since it was the General opinion, not only of Congress, but all cool and considerate Men, that an impost was the only practicable means of procuring money to pay the Interest of our foreign Debt, and that it is the most easy and equitable mode of raising a revenue.[24]

Congress's requisition system was "a burden too unequal and grievous for this State to submit to."[25]

The legislature met in special session in February 1786. Clark drafted both the resolution responding to Congress's requisition and the instructions to New Jersey's congressional delegation, employing some of the same arguments presented in his letter. New Jersey would not honor the requisition until the impost was approved. And, until the impost was approved, the state's congressional delegation was to vote against any expense unless the measure benefited either New Jersey or the entire union.

Congress was shocked. In March Charles Pinckney (South Carolina), Nathaniel Gorham (Massachusetts), and William Grayson (Virginia) were dispatched to plead with the legislature to reconsider. Pinckney painted a gloomy picture of the consequences of New Jersey's stand should the legislature remain recalcitrant.

> Perhaps I do not go too far in asserting, that a perseverance in your refusal, may afford them this opportunity, by dissolving those ties which bind us as a nation: for should the other states suspend their supplies, to the common treasury, until New Jersey complies with the requisition, the existence of the federal government must be endangered—probably cease....
> Let us for a moment suppose the confederation dissolved, and

an assembly of the states convened for the purpose of adopting a system calculated to render the general government firm and energetic—is it not to be reasonably expected, that the large states would contend and insist upon a greater influence than they at present possess?... It ought, therefore, to appear exceedingly important to the small states to maintain a system so advantageous to their particular interests.[26]

He did suggest that a proper remedy for the perceived inadequacy of the Articles might be a state call for a general convention to amend them. The legislature discussed the matter for three days before it agreed to rescind the February resolution. It continued to insist that the requisition system was unreasonable. The legislature's change of heart was more cosmetic than real. New Jersey took no steps to comply with the requisition. Indeed, no state made any attempt to supply the requisitioned funds. By June 1786 Congress was nearly out of money.

New Jersey's rebellion lent considerable weight to calls for some reform of the Articles. Congress had coped as best it could with the unwieldy requisition system. New Jersey's refusal to comply with a system which it perceived as grossly unfair made the fragility of the union apparent.

Annapolis

Virginia's invitation to a September 1786 convention in Annapolis to discuss Congress's power over trade followed closely on New Jersey's refusal to honor the requisition. New Jersey sent three representatives—Abraham Clark, William Churchill Houston, and James Schureman—and equipped them with liberal instructions. The trio was authorized to examine trade of the individual states and the United States, and to consider a uniform system of trade regulation—and "other important Matters."

Toward a New Nation

It was an interesting delegation. Clark was an advocate of some expansion of Congress's authority and was particularly concerned about the economic domination of New Jersey by New York and Pennsylvania.

Houston (1746–1788) was a prominent lawyer whose specialties were tax and financial questions. He was a Princeton graduate and, like many prominent New Jerseyans, a Presbyterian. Houston was a member of the New Jersey assembly from 1777 to 1779 and of Congress intermittently from 1779 to 1785. He served as clerk of the New Jersey supreme court from 1781 to his death. He advocated the taxation of luxuries and of slavery, an institution he opposed. Houston was appointed a delegate to both the Annapolis and Constitutional conventions. There is some doubt as to his attendance at either, since he was suffering from advanced tuberculosis.

Schureman (1756–1824), a product of Queen's College, was a prominent New Brunswick merchant. He served as a militia officer during the war. He was a member of the New Jersey assembly from 1783 to 1785 and in 1788, and he was a delegate to Congress in 1786–87. Schureman was a determined opponent of all paper-money measures. A staunch Federalist, he represented New Jersey in both the House and the Senate under the new Constitution.

Delegations from New Jersey, Virginia, New York, Delaware and Pennsylvania attended, but no delegation arrived with the same instructions. Delegates from New Hampshire, Rhode Island, Massachusetts and North Carolina did not arrive in time; the other states ignored the convention.

Scant attendance and disparate instructions precluded any close examination of a uniform system of trade regulation. Balked from a discussion of the specifics, the delegates turned to a consideration of the general. Alexander Hamilton, who was most anxious to achieve a restructuring of the national government, was bound by the New York legislature's strict instructions to its delegates to consider only matters of trade. He could not officially propose a wide-ranging examination of the structure of government. Abraham Clark, however, was in no such difficulty. He had been given a free hand by the New Jersey legislature, a body that hoped desperately for major reform. Clark offered a resolution calling for a constitutional convention in May 1787.

After some debate over the wisdom of such a bold move, the convention issued a report in line with Clark's resolution and Hamilton's fondest wish. The report called for a convention in Philadelphia in May and noted that

> the Idea of extending the powers of their Deputies, to other objects than those of Commerce which has been adopted by the State of New Jersey, was an improvement on the original plan, and will deserve to be incorporated into that of a future Convention.... [T]he power of regulating trade is of such comprehensive extent, and will enter so far into the general System of the foederal government, that to give it efficacy, and to obviate questions and doubts concerning its precise nature and limits may require a correspondent adjustment of other parts of the Foederal System.[27]

Congress approved the recommendation in February 1787.

New Jersey, Pennsylvania, Virginia, Delaware and North Carolina named delegates to the Constitutional Convention before Congress even endorsed the idea. Massachusetts, New York, Georgia, South Carolina, Maryland, Connecticut and New Hampshire selected delegates between February and June. Rhode Island, in keeping with its highly individualistic approach to all issues, ignored the convention.

Shays's Rebellion

Alarm over the possible spread of the kind of agrarian unrest which had afflicted Massachusetts from July 1786 to

February 1787 may have spurred some states to choose delegates quickly.

In July 1786 the Massachusetts General Court adjourned without agreeing on measures to relieve the debt-ridden farmers of the state. By then the number of foreclosures for debt had risen alarmingly. Discontent increased, particularly in western Massachusetts, which was the most severely afflicted area.

In August and September armed men prevented courts from sitting in Northampton, Worcester, Concord and Great Barrington—an effective method of preventing more foreclosures. The governor dispatched the state militia to Springfield to protect the superior court. Daniel Shays, an impoverished farmer, led some five hundred equally distressed men who confronted the militia and forced the court to adjourn. Congress, thoroughly alarmed (a federal arsenal was located in Springfield) authorized the formation of a force of thirteen hundred men, on the pretext of a supposed Indian menace. For its part the state, which had not exerted itself to address the farmers' problems, bestirred itself and enlisted four thousand men to crush Shays and his luckless followers. Shays's disorganized force, which had grown to twelve hundred, could not contend with the state militia, and the rebellion collapsed in February 1787.

Shays and his followers may or may not have posed a genuine threat. However, the specter of armed Americans in rebellion against governments so lately established and at such cost did have a salutary effect. The Massachusetts legislators made more conscientious efforts to address the farmers' plight and finally enacted some of the same measures New Jersey had. Congress was frightened into action, though its hastily authorized force was not used. Most important, the example of Shays's Rebellion lent new urgency to the call for reform of the Articles.

Philadelphia

The Constitutional Convention opened May 25, 1787. New Jersey had named as delegates David Brearly, William Paterson, William Churchill Houston and John Neilson. Neilson declined the appointment, but cited no reason, and Houston's health made choosing a replacement desirable. William Livingston and Abraham Clark were named as replacements. Clark declined on the grounds that he was already serving as a congressman, and Jonathan Dayton replaced him.

Brearly (1745–1790) was a prominent lawyer who had helped draft the New Jersey constitution in 1776. He was the chief justice of the New Jersey supreme court from 1779 to 1789 and a judge of the United States District Court from 1789 until his death. Brearly was an Episcopalian and had served as a lieutenant colonel in the war. A strong opponent of paper money, he became a Federalist and later served as a presidential elector in the first federal election.

Dayton (1760–1824), a graduate of the College of New Jersey and a member of a wealthy family, was one of the youngest men at the convention. He had served as a captain during the Revolution, but his military career was marred by occasional imprudence. He was captured once, and rumors circulated about his involvement in smuggling. Dayton owned a large number of public securities and was an enthusiastic land speculator. At the convention he was a vigorous defender of the rights of small states. Though considered a protege of Abraham Clark, Dayton became a Federalist.

Paterson became the most important member of the New Jersey delegation, though all five men went on to hold important state or federal office under the new Constitution.

The delegates to the Philadelphia convention faced no easy

task. First, they had to reach agreement on how radically to reform the Articles. Further, they had to achieve consensus on the authority to be given the central government and on how the states might be protected both from each other and from the central government.

The convention considered two plans of government, one from Virginia, the other from New Jersey. Virginia's proposal completely restructured the government but ensured the dominance of large states. New Jersey's counterproposal rearranged the elements of the Confederation and placed all states on an equal footing.

On May 29 Governor Edmund Randolph of Virginia presented a series of resolutions known as the Virginia plan. Randolph proposed a government of three branches—legislative, executive and judicial. The legislature would be bicameral with proportional representation. The lower house would be elected by the people; the upper house would be selected by the lower from a slate of nominees proposed by the state legislatures. The legislature would choose the executive, who would serve a single term, as well as members of the judiciary, who would serve on good behavior. At least one supreme court and a system of inferior courts would make up the judicial branch. A council of revision, consisting of the executive and several members of the judiciary, would have a veto on the legislature.

Randolph's plan dramatically increased the power of the legislature. The legislature had authority in all cases where the separate states were not competent, a broad area which included clear authority to raise revenue. It could nullify any state law infringing on the powers of the national government. Until the convention amended Randolph's proposals, the plan gave the legislature the authority to nullify any state law.

The judicial branch had jurisdiction in maritime matters, cases involving foreigners, the collection of the national rev-

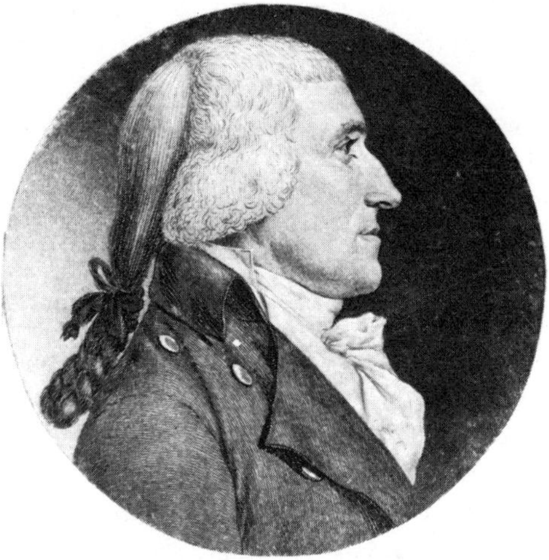

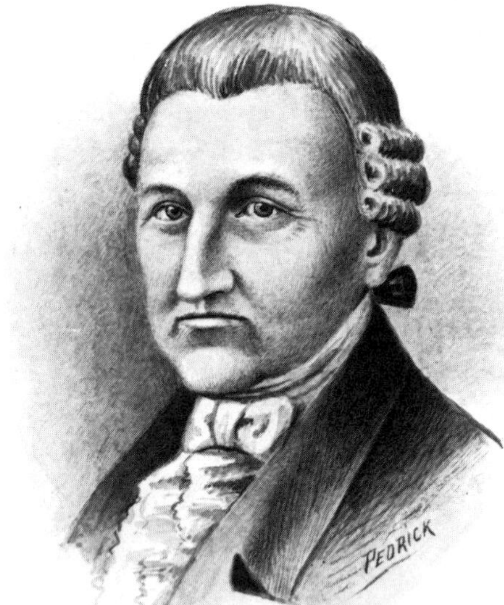
PEDRICK

enue, the impeachment of national officials and the general peace and harmony of the union.

The small states found the Virginia plan objectionable because it put states with small populations at a distinct disadvantage. The large states would control both houses of the legislature and consequently the choice of the executive and the members of the judiciary.

The convention debated Randolph's plan for two weeks, until an amended version won approval on June 13. Two days later William Paterson presented the small-state response, which was based on a reform of the Articles rather than an entirely new frame of government. Paterson's plan retained equal representation for all states. It authorized Congress to regulate foreign and interstate commerce and gave it limited taxation powers. Acts of Congress and United States treaties would be the supreme law of the land.

The plan proposed a plural executive with powers similar to those outlined by Randolph's plan, but gave it no veto. A supreme court, appointed by the executive, had original jurisdiction in cases of impeachment and appellate jurisdiction from state courts in maritime cases, cases involving foreigners, treaties, and acts concerning the regulation of trade or the collection of the federal revenue.

New Jersey's plan provided specific remedies for the deficiencies first noted in 1778. The power to tax and to regulate commerce would provide Congress a secure source of revenue, free the states from the inequitable and unworkable requi-

Jonathan Dayton, by Charles B. J. Fevret de Saint Memin. National Portrait Gallery, Smithsonian Institution.

David Brearly. William S. Sharp Collection, Special Collections and Archives, Alexander Library, Rutgers University.

sition method of finance, and prohibit one state from exacting import duties from the citizens of another. Moreover, making federal law and United States treaties supreme would provide an effective method of solving disputes between states, such as the western lands question, and would enable Congress to negotiate commercial treaties with foreign powers.

New Jersey's delegation was actually responsible for two proposals in support of equal representation. David Brearly suggested that all existing state boundaries be redrawn, providing for thirteen precisely equal states. The convention made approving noises about the desirability of equitable boundaries but took no action.

The convention debated the Paterson plan for three days before rejecting it in favor of a renewed consideration of the Virginia plan. However, the small states continued to oppose proportional representation because it embodied some of their worst fears about the domination of small by large states. On July 16 the convention broke the stalemate when it accepted Connecticut delegate Roger Sherman's compromise calling for a two-house legislature. Representation in one house would be based on population (all whites and three-fifths of the black population); in the other house each state would receive equal representation. The three-fifths compromise was a sop to the South.

Once New Jersey was assured of some form of equal representation, its delegation found the new Constitution a suitable frame of government because it provided useful solutions to problems New Jersey had first cited in 1778.

A committee on detail refined the convention's rough draft of twenty-three resolutions and presented the document for consideration on August 6. The final draft was prepared and presented for approval on September 12. On September 17 the document was approved by each of the twelve state delegations and signed by thirty-nine of forty-two delegates present. Only George Mason and Edmund Randolph of Virginia and Elbridge Gerry of Massachusetts refused to sign.

The form of government the convention produced owed more to Virginia's contribution than New Jersey's. Paterson's scheme rearranged the elements of the Confederation; Randolph's restructured the government. Still, New Jersey's contribution was a significant one. The state legislature's exasperation with the Confederation's mode of finance had finally led to the flat refusal to comply with the requisition of funds. This stand certainly encouraged the states that sent delegations to Annapolis. New Jersey's broad instructions to its Annapolis delegates were cited as a model, and the New Jersey plan provided a useful corrective to the Virginia plan.

Congress received the document on September 20, 1787. Richard Henry Lee (Virginia) and Melancton Smith (New York) argued that the thirteenth article of the Articles of Confederation permitted Congress to amend the Articles, not to construct an entirely new frame of government. Lee, who believed the new government to be too powerful, proposed that the document be amended before forwarding it to the states for ratification. Lee's proposal, which listed a number of basic rights, incorporated a provision for a second convention. If passed, the proposal might well have consigned the Constitution to defeat. The majority in Congress favored sending the Constitution to the states with Congress's approval. Lee, among others, would have voted in the negative. Advocates of the Constitution were afraid to send the document forth with any appearance of a negative. On September 28 it was resolved to forward the document to the states without citing Congress's opinion. To give the appearance of approbation, if not the reality, the Constitution's supporters made sure the resolution stated that the document was being forwarded unanimously. Ratification required the assent of nine states. Advocates of the Constitution probably hoped the appearance of unanimity would sway some states.

Abraham Clark, who has been cited as the closest thing

in New Jersey to an Antifederalist, was not enthusiastic about the Constitution. Lack of enthusiasm did not lead to organized opposition. In July 1788, ten months after Congress had considered the new Constitution, Clark explained his position in a letter to a prosperous Salem merchant, Thomas Sinnickson. Clark conceded that he had "never liked the System in all its parts," believing it "more a Consolidated government than a federal, a government too expensive, and unnecessarily Oppressive in its Opperation." However, he asserted that he

> nevertheless wished it to go to the States from Congress just as it did, without any Censure or Commendation, hoping that in Case of a general Adoption, the Wisdom of the States would soon amend it in the exceptional parts. Strong fears however remained upon my mind untill I found the Custom of Recommending amendments with the Adoptions began to prevail. This set my mind at ease.... [Y]ou will readily conclude I anxiously wish every state may come into the adoption in order to effect a measure with me so desirable; in which case, from the general current of amendments proposed, we shall retain all the important parts in which New Jersey is interested.[28]

Ratification

The Philadelphia convention's handiwork became public knowledge quickly. The text of the Constitution appeared in *The Trenton Mercury* and in a New Brunswick broadside on September 25.

In the first three weeks of October the legislature received several petitions from citizens of Salem, Middlesex, Gloucester and Burlington counties calling for a ratifying convention. All indicated approval of the new frame of government. The most fervent was one from Salem, which read in part,

> We are convinced, after the most serious and unprejudiced examination of the different articles and sections of articles of the Constitu-

tion, that nothing but the immediate adoption of it can save the United States in general, and this state in particular, from absolute ruin.[29]

On October 8 Lambert Cadwallader, a New Jersey delegate to the Confederation Congress, wrote to Delaware delegate George Mitchell assessing the Constitution and its chances for ratification. Cadwallader found "the proposed new Federal Constitution ... a very excellent one [which] ... will make us if adopted happy at home and respectable abroad." He foresaw no opposition in New Jersey and looked forward to "the prospect of better times ... if we are wise enough to take the boon that is offered us." Cadwallader happily considered America's improved standing among foreign nations which the new frame of government would mean.

> We shall derive prodigious advantages from the regulation of our trade with foreign powers who have taken the opportunity of our feeble state to turn everything to their own benefit. By playing off one nation against another we may bring them one after the other to some consideration for us, which they have not had for some years past. They have sacrificed our interest in every instance to their own in full expectation of our inability to counteract them.[30]

New Jersey was quick to select delegates to a ratifying convention. In late October Congress authorized the states to call their own ratifying conventions. On October 23, the legislature convened in Trenton. The October 1787 election campaign had focused on state issues, not the Constitution. The makeup of council and assembly changed very little.

On October 25 the county petitions were read in the assembly, followed by Governor Livingston's message presenting the text of the Constitution, the resolution of the Constitutional Convention, and Congress's resolution transmitting the Constitution to the states. On October 26 three of New Jersey's four convention delegates presented their own reports to the legislature.

Toward a New Nation

By October 29 both houses passed unanimous resolutions calling for a state ratifying convention. For good measure they also passed a bill making the convention legal.

The election of the thirty-nine delegates was without incident, and on December 11 they convened in a Trenton tavern, the Blazing Star. Most of the delegates had held civil or military office during the Revolution and were prominent in their communities. Service in the assembly or council (royal or state), or the Continental Congress figured prominently in their careers. The majority had not been politically active during the preceding three years. Most had substantial estates. Twelve were professionals of one sort or another, four were engaged in the iron industry, and the rest were landowners. Few held large amounts of state or Continental securities.[31]

Information about the convention's deliberations is scanty. *The Trenton Mercury* on December 18 published an account of the proceedings in very general terms. The delegates took three days to select officers, discuss the rules governing the convention and read both the legislature's authorizing resolution and the Constitution itself. They selected John Stevens, Sr., the wealthiest man present, as president. The post of secretary went to Samuel Witham Stockton, who was not a delegate but was a member of a prominent family. December 14, 15, and 17 were devoted to a reading of the Constitution section by section. On December 18 the Constitution was read again, debated and unanimously approved. A ceremonial procession to the courthouse for a public reading followed ratification. The celebration was punctuated by musket fire, thirteen rounds for the new nation and one each for Delaware and Pennsylvania, which had ratified before New Jersey.

Seeking a more convivial expression of their satisfaction with the completed task, the convention delegates repaired to Mr. Vandergrift's tavern. According to the account printed in *The Trenton Mercury*, the joy of the occasion was fixed

The site of New Jersey's ratifying convention. From Carlos E. Godfrey, The Mechanics Bank, 1834–1919 *(1919).*

This is a twentieth-century representation of a Trenton tavern at King and Second streets (now South Warren and West State). During the 1780s the tavern had several different owners and operated under a variety of names, among them the French Arms, the City Tavern and the Blazing Star. The New Jersey Legislature, the Continental Congress, and the ratifying convention all met here. At the time of the ratifying convention the tavern's proprietor was Francis Witt, who called it the Blazing Star.

Toward a New Nation

in every heart and expressed with liquid abandon. Sober reflection gave way, at least temporarily, to extended celebration. The assembled group downed at least thirteen toasts, including salutes to the Constitution; the United States in Congress; the perpetuity of the Union's independence; princes and states in alliance with the United States; "the interest of the United States ... ever ... the interest of each state"; those who had fallen; "religion, learning, the arts, manufactures, and commerce, in harmony and in mutual subserviency to each other"; the daughters of America; and America, "the asylum of invaded liberty."[32]

The convention adjourned on December 19, 1787, after passing a final resolution promoting a site in New Jersey as the nation's capital. Several months later the New Jersey legislature, responding to the convention's call, offered a site near Trenton for the new federal capital. New Jersey's hopes were unrewarded.

There is no evidence of any substantial opposition to the Constitution in New Jersey. Elias Boudinot, in a letter to William Bradford, Jr., of Pennsylvania, assessed the situation:

> I ... am rejoiced to find that the new Constitution is like to go down with you [Pennsylvania] on any terms. I am clear in it that some government is better than none and believe with you that there is now no alternative; but indeed when I consider the difficulty of reconciling thirteen jarring interests, and that in points of essential consequence, I confess it is better than I expected. It will not meet with any opposition in this state, but it gives universal satisfaction as far as I can judge.[33]

None of the commentaries from beyond the state's borders had indicated any doubt that New Jersey would ratify quickly. The *Pennsylvania Gazette* had reported on October 10, 1787, that a recent traveler in New Jersey had "met but *one* man who was opposed to it, and he was a citizen of Pennsylvania and an intimate friend of the head of the Antifederal Junto."

Toward a New Nation

This item was reprinted seventeen times from New Hampshire to Georgia by November 20.[34]

The state was equally prompt in ratifying the Bill of Rights. The issue of a bill of rights, a topic of hot debate elsewhere, seems to have been of minor interest to most New Jerseyans during ratification. As the New Jersey convention prepared to ratify, the *New Jersey Journal* printed a reply to George Mason's "Objections to the Constitution," which had appeared in the same paper on December 12, 1787. In part the reply dismissed the proposed bill of rights as unnecessary, observing

> every man of common sense would say that the people, or the sovereign power, cannot be affected by any such declaration of rights, they being the source of all power in the government; whatever they have not given away still remains inherent in them.[35]

Most of the debate in other states over the Constitution took place after New Jersey had ratified. The bill of rights question resurfaced during Virginia's consideration of the Constitution in the spring of 1788. Virginia was an important state with a considerable number of Antifederalists. Patrick Henry held up ratification for some time by citing the specter of oppression by an omnipotent national government, until George Wythe suggested a compromise of forwarding the ratified document accompanied by a list of rights that ought to be added.

The new Congress convened in April 1789 and occupied itself until the end of May with selection of officers, determination of the rules and other housekeeping chores. At the end of May, James Madison proposed nineteen amendments which he had carefully distilled from more than two hundred proffered by the state delegations. The House spent the summer debating the proposals and approved a modified version on August 4, 1789. The Senate followed suit in early

September. Congress forwarded twelve amendments to the states for ratification on September 25. Ten of the amendments were ratified by the states and became the Bill of Rights. New Jersey ratified first, on November 20.

Fighting Again

During the summer of congressional debate over the Bill of Rights, New Jersey was distracted by public excitement over its disputed congressional election.

In October 1788 the council had appointed a committee to draft a plan for electing United States senators, representatives and presidential electors. Governor and privy council selected the six presidential electors; assembly and council the first senators. The choices, William Paterson and Jonathan Elmer for the Senate and David Brearly, James Kinsey, John Neilson, David Moore, John Rutherfurd and Matthias Ogden as electors, were all impeccable Federalists.

The procedures for selecting members of the House of Representatives were more cumbersome. The legislature decided that representatives should be chosen at large rather than by district, and then approved a complicated nomination procedure. Any qualified voter could nominate four candidates for representative simply by delivering the list to the clerk of his county court of common pleas. The clerk forwarded the names to the governor for publication. The polls opened on the second Wednesday in February; no closing date was set. The governor and privy council counted the ballots and determined the winners. In addition, the legislature increased the number of polling places, a move of special importance for more sparsely populated West Jersey.

The election was fiercely contested, outrageously corrupt and a model of the aggressive party politics to come. West Jersey leaders, with the support of a few key figures in East

Jersey, combined to place in nomination a single slate of four opponents of paper money. This so-called Junto ticket consisted of Elias Boudinot and James Schureman of East Jersey and Thomas Sinnickson and Lambert Cadwallader of West Jersey. All were staunch Federalists, all were popular in West Jersey, and all but Sinnickson had served in the Continental Congress. Schureman alone had significant East Jersey support. East Jersey interests were not able to settle on one slate but nominated many men. Abraham Clark and Jonathan Dayton were nominated most frequently and became the major East Jersey candidates. Both Clark and Boudinot had been nominated for the Senate and lost. Dayton had some West Jersey support; Clark, because of his prodebtor stance, was anathema in the southern part of the state.

The campaign demonstrated New Jersey's sectional division at its most severe. Despite the fact that there had been no real opposition to the Constitution, the Junto pictured its candidates as sturdy upholders of the Constitution and thus deserving of support. Clark and Dayton were portrayed as enemies of the new government. Clark, Dayton and their adherents countered with charges that the Junto was composed of influential men devoted to intrigue. Various other charges circulated concerning past financial improprieties, voting records in the Confederation Congress and, most ludicrous, the major crime of hostility to General Washington.

Public vituperation was accompanied by energetic behind-the-scenes manipulation of the voting procedures. A Junto victory required at least one vote by nearly every available West Jersey voter. Election officials, controlled by the Junto, moved polls around the circuit twice, accepted votes cast in places not designated as polls, and refused ballots not marked with the prescribed four names. They persuaded Quakers to vote for the Junto by labeling Clark and Dayton as dangerous Presbyterians who were determined to oppress them. The seven northern counties closed their polls in late February showing healthy vote totals for Schureman, Clark and Dayton. Burlington, Cumberland and Gloucester counties promptly extended their polling period into March. Essex County countered by extending its polling period. New Jersey's polls finally closed on April 27.

The governor and council first met on March 3, 1789, after the close of polling in the seven northern counties, but they postponed any decision until the next meeting of the privy council on March 18. By then the election picture had changed considerably. A probable March 3 delegation of Schureman, Clark, Dayton and Boudinot had changed to a delegation of Schureman, Cadwallader, Boudinot and Sinnickson. With the Essex polls still open, the governor and council had results from just twelve of thirteen counties. Ignoring the sharp objections of council members from Morris, Somerset and Monmouth, Governor Livingston and the privy council declared the results of March 18 as final. Livingston forwarded the final decision to Congress, which promptly turned it over to its committee on elections. The committee heard testimony, but took no action. No doubt reluctant to begin a new government by unseating a state delegation, it simply forwarded a noncommittal report to the House. In September 1789 the House declared the Junto candidates to be duly elected.

New Jerseyans had been united on the Constitution because it presented solutions to problems which had plagued the state since independence. But the period of unanimity was brief. Sectional divisions had long been an important feature of political life. New Jersey's two regions were different economically, socially, religiously and ethnically. New Jerseyans were deeply divided over problems facing the state in the 1780s—debtor-creditor issues, the controversy over the loan office. The two regions agreed on little else but the deficiencies of the Confederation. For New Jerseyans, the Constitution represented the raft offered the drowning man. However, the contentiousness of the 1780s remained. Sectional differences reappeared in the first federal election and thereafter in the political struggles between Federalists and Jeffersonian Republicans.

Chronology

1776

21 June: New Jersey provincial congress votes to form a new government.
22 June: Provincial congress sends a new delegation of John Witherspoon, Richard Stockton, Abraham Clark, Francis Hopkinson and John Hart to the Continental Congress to vote for independence.
2 July: Congress votes for independence.
  Provincial congress adopts a new state constitution.
28 October: Battle of White Plains.
18 November–20 December: American troops retreat across New Jersey.
26 December: Battle of Trenton.

1777

3 January: Battle of Princeton.
15 November: Congress adopts the "Articles of Confederation and Perpetual Union."
17 December: France recognizes American independence.

1778

6 February: France forms an alliance with the United States.
12 April: Parliament appoints the Carlisle commission to negotiate with Congress. Congress rejects the idea of reconciliation and declines to negotiate.

Chronology

16 June: New Jersey legislature sends a "Representation" to Congress noting the deficiencies of the Articles.
28 June: Battle of Monmouth.
20 November: New Jersey ratifies the Articles of Confederation.

1779

21 June: Spain declares war on Great Britain but declines to recognize American independence.
14 August: Congress states its minimum peace terms: independence, removal of British troops, certain minimum boundaries, and free navigation of the Mississippi.

1780

1 February: New York cedes western land claims to the United States.
18 March: Congress resolves to replace the depreciated Continental currency with a more stable issue.
25 May: Mutiny at Washington's camp at Morristown.
21 September: Treason of Benedict Arnold.
10 October: Connecticut cedes western land claims (with the exception of reserved lands in the Ohio country) to the United States.

1781

1781–86: New Jersey legislature passes several measures to relieve its debtors. These efforts culminate in the passage of a loan office (paper money) bill in 1786.
1 January: Mutiny of the Pennsylvania Line at Morristown.
2 January: Virginia conditionally cedes her claims north of the Ohio River to the United States.

3 February: Congress asks the states for the authority to impose a 5 percent import tax.

20 February: Robert Morris is named superintendent of the newly created department of finance.

1 March: Final ratification of the Articles of Confederation.

25 May: New Jersey legislature agrees to the import tax. Rhode Island's negative in December 1782 defeats it.

14–15 June: Congress names John Jay, Benjamin Franklin, Henry Laurens and Thomas Jefferson to join John Adams on a peace negotiating commission.

18 October: General Charles Lord Cornwallis surrenders at Yorktown.

1782

Fall: New Jersey legislature debates the value of the new currency issued in 1780.

30 November: Preliminary articles of peace signed.

1783

20 January: Effective date of Articles of Peace.

15 April: Congress ratifies the Treaty of Paris.

18 April: Congress asks the states for authority to impose a 5 percent import tax and a supplemental revenue, each for a twenty-five year period. It also asks them to cede all remaining crown lands.

26 April: Last large group of Loyalists leave New York for Canada or Europe.

11 June: New Jersey legislature approves Congress's financial plan.

13 June: Army begins to disband.

24 June: Congress flees Philadelphia for Princeton just ahead of troops demanding back pay.

1784

August: Debate begins in New Jersey over the proposed loan office bill.

December: New Jersey legislature stops deliveries of money to the Continental treasury until all thirteen states approve the impost and the supplemental revenue.

1785

28 March: Representatives of Virginia and Maryland meet at Mount Vernon to discuss navigation of their common waterways. Subsequently, the Virginia legislature proposes that a conference on commercial problems be held in Annapolis.

July–August: Negotiations begin between the United States and Spain over the Florida–United States boundary and the free navigation of the Mississippi.

27 September: Congress issues a requisition for $3 million.

December–April 1786: Newspaper debate in New Jersey over the loan office bill.

1786

16 January: Virginia legislature adopts the statute on religious freedom.

20 February: New Jersey assembly resolves not to meet Congress's requisition until all thirteen states approve the impost and supplemental revenue.

13 March: Congressional delegation, headed by Charles Pinckney (SC), urges the New Jersey legislature to comply with the requisition. Legislature rescinds the February vote but never takes action on the requisition.

26 May: New Jersey legislature passes loan office bill.

August–December: Shays's Rebellion.

Chronology

11–14 September: Annapolis Convention.

23 November: New Jersey begins naming its delegation to the Philadelphia convention. The final delegation consists of David Brearly, William Paterson, William Livingston, Jonathan Dayton, and, possibly, William Churchill Houston.

1787

February: Shays's Rebellion crushed.

21 February: Congress approves the Philadelphia meeting, limiting its scope to revising the Articles of Confederation. New Jersey, Virginia, Pennsylvania, Delaware and North Carolina have already named delegations.

February–June: Massachusetts, New York, Georgia, South Carolina, Maryland, Connecticut and New Hampshire name delegates. Rhode Island ignores the convention.

25 May: Convention opens.

29 May: Edmund Randolph proposes the Virginia plan.

15 June: William Paterson proposes the New Jersey plan.

19 June: Convention reaffirms its decision to construct a new frame of government rather than amend the Articles of Confederation.

13 July: Congress passes the Northwest Ordinance providing for governance of territory north of the Ohio River.

16 July: Roger Sherman proposes the Connecticut compromise.

August–September: The convention debates the provisions of the Constitution.

17 September: The twelve attending state delegations (Rhode Island sent no delegation) approve the Constitution. Thirty-nine of forty-two delegates in attendance sign the document.

20 September: Congress receives the new Constitution.

Chronology

- 28 September: Congress resolves to submit the document to special state ratifying conventions.
- 27 October: First "Federalist" paper appears. Between October and May 1788 eighty-five articles, written by Alexander Hamilton, James Madison and John Jay under the name of "Publius," will appear in defense of the new Constitution.
- 7 December: Delaware ratifies.
- 12 December: Pennsylvania ratifies.
- 18 December: New Jersey ratifies.

1788

- 2 January–6 February: Georgia, Connecticut, and Massachusetts ratify.
- 24 March: Rhode Island rejects the Constitution. The state will not ratify until May 1790.
- 28 April–21 June: Maryland, South Carolina, and New Hampshire ratify. In accordance with Article 7, approval by the ninth state signals the adoption of the Constitution.
- 25 June–26 July: Virginia and New York ratify.
- 2 August: North Carolina withholds ratification. The state will ratify in September 1789 after Congress sends the states twelve amendments outlining basic individual rights.
- 25 November: The New Jersey assembly and council select William Paterson and Jonathan Elmer as New Jersey's first United States senators.

1789

- 7 January: Governor Livingston and the privy council select David Brearly, James Kinsey, John Neilson, David

Moore, John Rutherfurd and Matthias Ogden as presidential electors.

11 February–27 April: New Jersey votes in its first federal election. The election of James Schureman, Elias Boudinot, Thomas Sinnickson, and Lambert Cadwallader to the House is disputed.

4 March: The new Congress convenes in New York.

30 April: Washington is inaugurated as the first president under the new Constitution.

Summer: Congress considers the various amendments to the Constitution suggested by the state ratifying conventions.

27 July–24 September: Congress establishes the Department of Foreign Affairs (later renamed the Department of State), the War Department, the Treasury Department, and the office of Postmaster General, and passes the Federal Judiciary Act.

13 August: Committee on elections hears testimony about New Jersey's election.

September: House of Representatives declares Schureman, Boudinot, Sinnickson and Cadwallader duly elected.

9 September: Congress recommends the adoption of twelve amendments to the Constitution.

25 September: Congress submits twelve amendments to the states. Ten of these will be adopted and constitute the Bill of Rights.

20 November: New Jersey becomes the first state to ratify the Bill of Rights. On 15 December 1791 the Bill of Rights becomes part of the Constitution.

Notes

1. Merrill Jensen, ed. *The Documentary History of the Ratification of the Constitution*, I, pp. 115-16.
2. Edmund C. Burnett, ed., *Letters of Members of the Continental Congress* (Washington, 1926), 3:326-27.
3. Larry R. Gerlach, ed. *New Jersey in the American Revolution, 1763-1783: A Documentary History* (Trenton: New Jersey Historical Commission, 1975), p. 205.
4. Ibid., p. 303.
5. Ibid., p. 236.
6. Ibid., p. 299.
7. Ibid.
8. Ibid., pp. 266-67.
9. Richard P. McCormick, *Experiment in Independence: New Jersey In the Critical Period, 1781-1789* (New Brunswick: Rutgers University Press, 1950), p. 31.
10. John E. O'Connor, *William Paterson: Lawyer and Statesman, 1745-1806* (New Brunswick: Rutgers University Press, 1979), p. 121.
11. Ibid., p. 122.
12. "Primitive Whig," *New Jersey Gazette*, Jan. 9, 1786.
13. O'Connor, *Paterson*, pp. 123-24.
14. Abraham Clark, *The True Policy of New-Jersey, Defined* ... (Elizabeth-Town: Shepard Kollock, 1786), pp. 8-9, 11.
15. Ibid., p. 11.
16. *New Jersey Gazette*, Jan. 9, 1786.
17. *New Jersey Gazette*, Feb. 6, 1786.
18. Clark, *True-Policy*, p. 33.
19. *New Jersey Gazette*, Feb. 13, 1786.
20. O'Connor, *Paterson*, p. 124.
21. Clark, *True-Policy*, pp. 34-35.
22. Burnett, *Letters*, 7:348.
23. Eugene R. Sheridan and John M. Murrin, *Congress at Princeton: Being the Letters of Charles Thomson to Hannah Thomson, June-October 1783* (Princeton: Princeton University Library, 1985), pp. 72-73.
24. McCormick, *Experiment*, p. 237.
25. Ibid.
26. Burnett, *Letters*, 8:764-65.
27. Jensen, *Documentary History*, 1:183-84.

Notes

28. Burnett, *Letters*, 8:764–65.
29. Jensen, *Documentary History*, 3:136–37.
30. Ibid., pp. 137–38.
31. McCormick, *Experiment*, pp. 266–69.
32. Jensen, *Documentary History*, 3:189–90.
33. Ibid, p. 134.
34. Ibid., p. 140.
35. Ibid., p. 154.

Bibliographical Essay

In most cases I have footnoted only the sources of the quotations used in this pamphlet. The following materials have proved most helpful in the writing of this essay; the reader is encouraged to delve further into the subjects covered.

On the whole, neither New Jersey nor America in the 1780s—except, of course, for the Constitution—has attracted a great deal of scholarly attention. The major study of New Jersey during the Confederation period and of the state's position on the Constitution is Richard P. McCormick, *Experiment in Independence: New Jersey in the Critical Period, 1781-1789* (New Brunswick, 1950). McCormick's study, more than thirty-five years after its completion, is still the standard work in the field and so finely crafted that no one has ventured into the field since. This book is heavily based on it. For background on the Confederation period itself, I have relied upon Merrill Jensen's sympathetic view of the period, *The New Nation. A History of the United States During the Confederation, 1781-1789* (New York, 1958), and Forrest McDonald's entertaining *E Pluribus Unum: The Formation of the American Republic, 1776-1790* (Boston, 1965).

I have turned to the following for detailed information on various aspects of the Confederation period. Peter O. Wacker's *Land and People. A Cultural Geography of Preindustrial New Jersey; Origins and Settlement Patterns* (New Brunswick, 1975) provides considerable information on patterns of population, ethnicity, religion and land use in New Jersey, especially chapters 3–5. Chapters 1, 6, 12 and 13 of Jackson Turner Main's *Political Parties Before the Constitution* (Chapel Hill, 1973) and chapters 1, 3, and 6 of his *Social Structure of Revolutionary America* (Princeton, 1965) analyze the state's political and social structure and legislative voting patterns in considerable detail. Information on education and educational institutions was taken from Richard P. McCormick, *Rutgers: A Bicentennial History* (New Brunswick, 1966), chapters 1 and 2; Thomas Jefferson Wertenbaker's *Princeton, 1746–1896* (Princeton, 1946), chapters 2 and 3; Lawrence Cremin's companion volumes, *American Education: The Colonial Experience, 1607–1783* (New York, 1970), chapter 18, and *American Education: The National Experience, 1783–1876* (New York, 1980), chapter 5; and Barbara Solomon, *In the Company of Educated Women* (New Haven, 1985), especially chapters 1 and 2. Material on New Jersey's religious portrait is from pp. 7–14 of *Religion in New Jersey Life Before the Civil War*, ed. Mary R. Murrin (Trenton, 1985); the discussion of literary activity is based on McCormick, *Experiment*, chapter 3. Gregory E. Dowd, "Declaration of Dependence: War and Inequality in Revolutionary New Jersey, 1776–1815," *New Jersey History* 103 (Spring/Summer 1985), pp. 47–67, Arthur Zilversmit, *The First Emancipation: Abolition of Slavery in the North* (Chicago, 1967), pp. 215–29, and McCormick, pp. 63–67, form the basis for the discussion of the position of blacks and the sentiment for antislavery in New Jersey. Information on the political rights of women in postwar New Jersey comes from Mary Beth Norton, *Liberty's Daughters: The Revolutionary Experience of American Women, 1750–1800* (Boston, 1980).

Material on New Jersey's wartime devastation comes from *The Toll of Independence: Engagements and Battle Casualties of the American Revolution*, ed. Howard H. Peckham (Chicago, 1974); the discussion of the Loyalist problem is based on Paul H. Smith, "New Jersey Loyalists and the British 'Provincial' Corps in the War for Independence," *New Jersey History* 87 (1969), pp. 67–78; military information is based on James Kirby Martin and Mark Edward Lender, *A Respectable Army:*

Bibliographical Essay

The Military Origins of the Republic, 1763–1789 (Arlington, Ill., 1982), Mark E. Lender, "The Conscripted Line: The Draft in Revolutionary New Jersey," *New Jersey History* 103 (Spring/Summer 1985), pp. 23–45, and Alfred Hoyt Bill, *New Jersey and the Revolutionary War* (New Brunswick, 1964). *New Jersey in the American Revolution, 1763–1783: A Documentary History,* ed. Larry R. Gerlach (Trenton, 1975), proved a fertile source of quotations on New Jersey's wartime devastation and the viciousness of the patriot-loyalist conflict.

Those portions of the pamphlet dealing with currency finance and paper money are based primarily on E. James Ferguson, *The Power of the Purse: A History of American Public Finance, 1776–1790* (Chapel Hill, 1961), chapter 1–4; Donald Kemmerer, "The Colonial Loan Office System in New Jersey," *Journal of Political Economy* 47 (1939), pp. 867–74; Edward A. Fuhlbruegge, "New Jersey Finances During the American Revolution," *Proceedings of the New Jersey Historical Society* 55 (1937), pp. 167–90; Joseph A. Ernst, *Money and Politics in America, 1755–1775: a Study in the Currency Act of 1764 and the Political Economy of Revolution* (Chapel Hill, 1973), chapter 8; and Richard A. Lester, *Monetary Experiments: Early American and Recent Scandinavian* (Princeton, 1939; repr. 1970). Information on currency equivalents is derived from John J. McCusker, *Money-Exchange in Europe and America, 1600–1775: A Handbook* (Chapel Hill, 1978).

For information on the 1780s economy, major studies include John J. McCusker and Russell R. Menard, *The Economy of British America, 1607–1789* (Chapel Hill, 1985), especially chapter 9 and individual references in chapters 10–17, and Curtis P. Nettels, *The Emergence of a National Economy, 1775–1815* (New York, 1962).

The discussion of sectional rivalries is based on Joseph L. Davis, *Sectionalism in American Politics, 1774–1787* (Madison,

Bibliographical Essay

1977); Peter Onuf, *The Origins of the Federal Republic: Jurisdictional Controversies in the United States, 1775–1787* (Philadelphia, 1983), especially chapters 1, 2, 4 and 7; and selected portions of Thomas P. Abernethy, *Western Lands and the American Revolution* (New York, 1959). The section on the location of the capital is based on Lawrence Delbert Cress's delightful essay, "Whither Columbia? Congressional Residence and the Politics of the New Nation, 1776 to 1787," *William and Mary Quarterly*, 3rd ser., 32 (October 1975), pp. 47–67; *The Papers of Alexander Hamilton*, ed. Harold C. Syrett and Jacob Cooke (New York, 1962), 6:487; and *Congress at Princeton: Being the Letters of Charles Thomson to Hannah Thomson, June–October 1783*, ed. Eugene R. Sheridan and John M. Murrin (Princeton, 1985), pp. 72–73.

A variety of biographical sources proved to be fertile sources of information and quotations. Information on William Livingston was based on Dennis P. Ryan's essay in *The Governors of New Jersey, 1664–1974: Biographical Essays*, ed. Paul A. Stellhorn and Michael Birkner (Trenton, 1982), pp. 77–81. Material on William Paterson comes from John E. O'Connor, *William Paterson, Lawyer and Statesman, 1745–1806* (New Brunswick, 1979), and the essay in James McLachlan, *Princetonians, 1748–1768: A Biographical Dictionary* (Princeton, 1975), pp. 437–40. Biographical information on Abraham Clark is based on Ruth Bogin, *Abraham Clark and the Quest for Equality in the Revolutionary Era, 1774–1794* (Rutherford, NJ, 1982). Richard A. Harrison, *Princetonians, 1776–1783: A Biographical Dictionary* (Princeton, 1981), pp. 31–42, was the source for material on Jonathan Dayton. The McLachlan volume of *Princetonians*, pp. 643–47, was the source for William Churchill Houston. David Brearly's life is not well documented; a rather thin sketch is contained in volume 3 of the *Dictionary of American Biography*. Material on James Schureman is from the *Biographical Directory of the American Congress, 1774–1971*.

Bibliographical Essay

Edmund C. Burnett's edition of the *Letters of Members of the Continental Congress* (Washington, DC, 1934; repr. 1963), volumes 7 and 8, proved a rich source of documentary material on a variety of issues facing the Confederation. Three volumes of Merrill Jensen's edition of *The Documentary History of the Ratification of the Constitution* (Madison, 1976–) contained a rich array of materials employed in this pamphlet. The three volumes were *Constitutional Documents and Records, 1776–1787* (vol. 1); *Ratification of the Constitution By the States Delaware, New Jersey, Georgia, Connecticut* (vol. 3); and *Commentaries on the Constitution: Public and Private, 21 February to 7 November 1787* (vol. 13). The New Jersey Historical Commission's William Livingston Papers project, under the editorship of Carl E. Prince at New York University, kindly provided me with copies and transcripts of the Primitive Whig essays from the *New Jersey Gazette*. The anonymous pamphlet, *The True Policy of New-Jersey, Defined; Or, Our Great Strength Led to Exertion, In the Improvement of Agriculture & Manufactures, By Altering the Mode of Taxation And by the Emission of Money on Loan* (Elizabeth-Town, 1786), which Ruth Bogin has conclusively identified as the work of Abraham Clark, is in the Special Collections Department, Alexander Library, Rutgers University.